"Brava to Claire Sierra for her brave and
Path. I am proud to call her my sister or

— Kathleen McGowan, autho
The E

"Claire Sierra has composed a marvelous tapestry of insights, discoveries, tools, and resources for all of us to use in designing a new global culture. The wisdom of the Magdalene informs and guides her journey and gives us all hope for Heaven on Planet Earth."

— Rev. Ruth L. Miller, PhD, author of *Mary's Power,*
The New Game of Life and *The Library of Hidden Knowledge*

"Balancing the forces of the masculine and feminine is the key task of our time; our future as a society depends on it. One of the key obstacles to achieving this balance, individually and collectively, is our culture's complete ignorance of the Divine Feminine. Claire's deep work with Sacred Feminine wisdom has brought to light a message of hope that couldn't come at a better time."

— Tim Kelley, author of *True Purpose* and
founder of the True Purpose™ Institute

"Claire brings forth the voice of the Magdalene with clarity and Divine Feminine purpose. She weaves ancient sacred knowledge with creative expression in potent ways that support the journey of women today. You will find Soul expanding insights in these pages."

— Lisa Michaels, author of *Natural Rhythms* and
Elemental Forces of Creation Oracle Cards

"*The Magdalene Path* is an important contribution to mending a world torn in half by the religions that rejected the Divine Feminine and buried her power. We are finally able to re-open that channel and find balance and wholeness, combining the divinity of the Masculine with the Feminine into a Divine Marriage. Claire Sierra was surprised to find Mary Magdalene speaking to her in meditation. She brings a fresh, clean and humble approach to this crucial quest. This book could have been called "Conversations with Goddess." *The Magdalene Path* is a graceful introduction to the mysteries of the true feminine: the gentle, fierce, fullness of the Goddess herself. As Magdalene reports to the author, *"Women are now ready to reveal their true divinity to themselves and to the world. And the world needs all these self-expressed, inspired, confident, love-filled women, ready to live as forces to be reckoned with. The world is ready. Prepare yourself. This wind is gathering power and coming your way."*

– Lion Goodman, author of *Creating on Purpose*,
creator of the Belief Closet Process ™ and
founder of the Luminary Leadership Institute

The Magdalene Path
Awaken the Power of Your Feminine Soul

CLAIRE SIERRA

BALBOA
PRESS
A DIVISION OF HAY HOUSE

Copyright © 2014 Claire Sierra.
Cover Image: © Sacred Dreamer by Claire Sierra, 2014

All rights reserved. No part of this book may be used or reproduced by any means, graphic, electronic, or mechanical, including photocopying, recording, taping or by any information storage retrieval system without the written permission of the publisher except in the case of brief quotations embodied in critical articles and reviews.

Balboa Press books may be ordered through booksellers or by contacting:

Balboa Press
A Division of Hay House
1663 Liberty Drive
Bloomington, IN 47403
www.balboapress.com
1-(877) 407-4847

Because of the dynamic nature of the Internet, any web addresses or links contained in this book may have changed since publication and may no longer be valid. The views expressed in this work are solely those of the author and do not necessarily reflect the views of the publisher, and the publisher hereby disclaims any responsibility for them.

The author of this book does not dispense medical advice or prescribe the use of any technique as a form of treatment for physical, emotional, or medical problems without the advice of a physician, either directly or indirectly. The intent of the author is only to offer information of a general nature to help you in your quest for emotional and spiritual well-being. In the event you use any of the information in this book for yourself, which is your constitutional right, the author and the publisher assume no responsibility for your actions.

Any people depicted in stock imagery provided by Thinkstock are models, and such images are being used for illustrative purposes only.
Certain stock imagery © Thinkstock.

Printed in the United States of America.

ISBN: 978-1-4525-6185-1 (sc)
ISBN: 978-1-4525-6186-8 (e)

Balboa Press rev. date: 10/23/2013

Dedication

To all my sisters who are hungering for the new mysteries of the Divine Feminine and are calling this forth, I bow and welcome you, one priestess to another. Blessed be.

Table of Contents

Dedication v

In Gratitude xi

Sacred Dreamer xv

Welcome 1

Chapter 1:   Magdalene Messages 11

Chapter 2:   Herstory 37

Chapter 3:   The Path of the Divine Feminine 81

Chapter 4:   Sacred Partnership 111

Chapter 5:   Embodying Feminine Essence 129

Chapter 6:   Lessons for Living Larger 161

Chapter 7:   Tools for the Path 185

Chapter 8:   Conclusion 211

Appendix 1: Re-visioning Mary Magdalene 225

Resources 235

Reference 237

About the Author 241

The Practices

A Note 83

Feed the Feminine First 84

Stepping into Feminine Leadership 89

Goddessing 92

Align from Your Purpose 97

Living from Being 103

Defining Feminine and Masculine 114

Vision Map 125

Be Your Beauty 132

Shine Your Light 135

Body Prayer 138

Cycle Awareness 142

Sacred Creativity of *Consecreation* 147

Create Your Temple Home 153

Rev-Up Your Holy Desire 163

Roll Out the Red Carpet 167

Gratitude Journal 171

Heart Dream Meditation 174

Creating Heaven on Planet Earth 182

Prayer Beads 187

Energy Bridge 189

Candle Magic 194

LightBreath Meditation 195

Open Your God Line 199

Magdalene Blessing 205

In Gratitude

I could fill pages with the names and stories of those who have helped, supported, inspired and conspired with me on this project for many years. Some came years before this book, some are arriving just as these pixels turn to ink. Please know that if I omit your name, you are still gold in my heart.

In her great wisdom, my dear buddy Jen Kelley astutely noted that the perfect solutions and/or people were showing up at the perfect time, including book mavens Elizabeth Marshall and Bobbye Middendorf. The Balboa/Hay House team used skill and savvy to create the book you hold in your hands. Carol Venolia's brilliance as an editor is paralleled by her intuitive instinct and unerring kindness. Tomar Levine, Erin Delaney, Martha Shonkwiler, Myrica Morningstar, Katharine Lee, Mar Goodman, Marcy Tilton and Monique DeJong were angelic evidence of Divine timing with support, feedback and constructive editing. My Spiritual Marketing Quest Platinum Mastermind and Power Circle sisters steadfastly encouraged me to see and reveal my truth, even when I felt otherwise. Marcy Tilton and Kate Dwyer sustained me with nourishment of all kinds through years of darkness and confusion before I was ready to birth this light. My dear Takilma Moon Circle Sisters: Roxy, Beth, Joya, Kate, Kathryn, Marilyn, Jen, Linda, Mary and Cathy, were part of a living laboratory to explore feminine wisdom through many cycles of the moon and sun.

No work in the Divine Feminine would be complete without the Divine Masculine. I am indebted to the amazing men in my life, particularly Ricardo Sierra with whom the initial sparks of this work began and Yogesh Zito, who taught me volumes about spirit connection, presence and compassion. My Manifesting Our Divine Purpose mastermind buddies: Lion, Hardy and John, taught me as much about the Divine Feminine as any women ever could.

Deep bows of to my many teachers through the years, including Tim Kelley and the late great Tamara Slayton. To Kathleen McGowan for sharing an incredible spiritual adventure into the heart of La Madeleine and for pivotal wisdom and direction, when I needed it most. To Margaret Starbird, Flo Aveia Magdalena, along with many writers, artists, initiates and scholars who have gone before for me, for lighting this Magdalene Path. I feel immense and infinite appreciation for my first teachers, my parents, Phyllis and Ray DiPietro and the lineage I carry through them. They may not always understand me, but they love me nonetheless.

Finally, there are no words to express the great gratitude I have for my beloved Josiah Dean, a true charming prince, who has supported this project with time, talent and treasure beyond compare. I can't imagine where I would be without you, nor do I want to.

Ultimately, I am humbled in gratitude to my Spirit team, for the gift of awakening this Magdalene Path that I carry, and of course, Mary Magdalene for her steadfast guidance and effervescent inspiration, encouraging me from the ethers. May her name be restored to the high holiness she deserves.

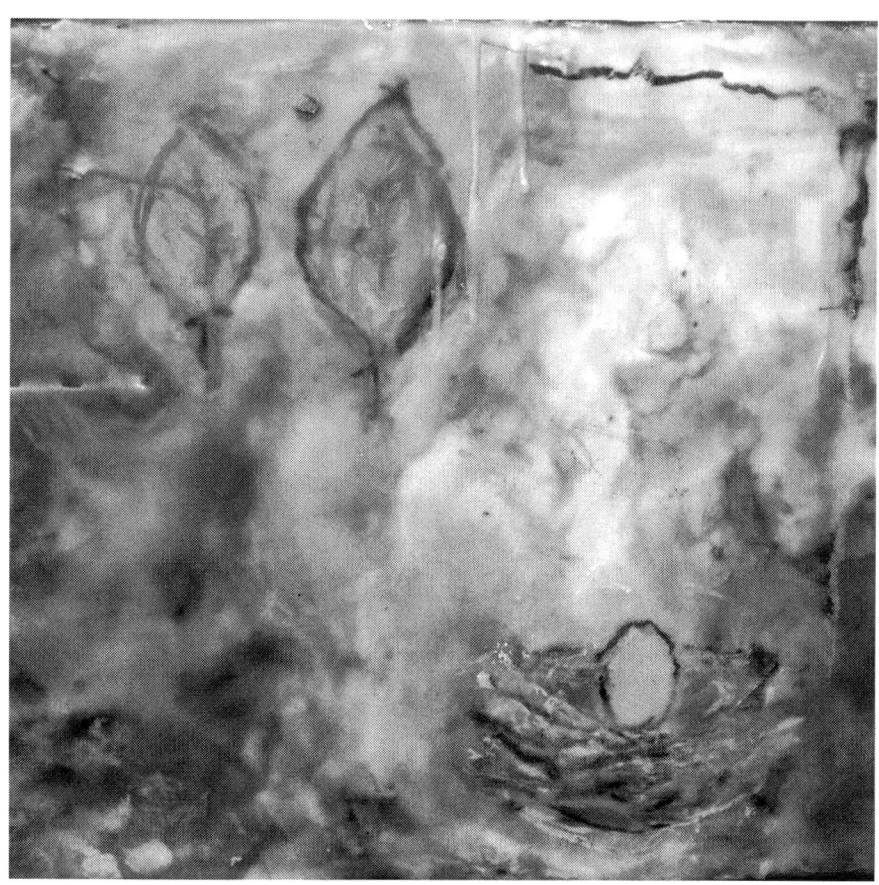

Home © 2014 Claire Sierra

Sacred Dreamer

Listen within to the Beauty of your Soul.

The Sacred treasures that lie deep within,

glistening like gemstones, are the stars that chart your course.

Follow this Mystery.

Allow your great unfolding (emerging, expanding, evolutionary Presence)

To the Essence of you:

God/Goddess Divine.

And bow in recognition,

this Dreamer is you.

© Claire Sierra, MA

The Path, © 2014 Claire Sierra

Welcome

Listening to Spirit

Do you ever have things you just "know" about yourself or your life? I think we all do, whether we admit it or not. For a long time I've known I would write a book, but I wondered what it could be about for a very long time. Never did I expect such an incredible journey.

Several years ago, in autumn of 2009, I had an amazing experience. While deep in meditation in the middle of my monthly acupuncture treatment, I had a visitation (for lack of a better word) from Mary Magdalene. She appeared in my mind's eye and asked me to write this book about the untold story of her life and how it relates to the awakening of the Divine Feminine in women today. I was astounded, but looking back now, it makes sense. My life path had led me to that place; it didn't just happen overnight.

I'd been getting nudges from Spirit during meditation about writing a book for some time, but it took this one indelible experience for me to acknowledge it. Once Mary Magdalene came to me with her request, I knew this was something I needed to do. My purpose was appearing and I could finally step up, heed that calling, and follow through. It's been quite an adventure and this is the middle of the tale. Let me back up a bit and explain how this unfolded.

The Journey Begins

I was raised Catholic, so perhaps I was primed for a connection with Mary Magdalene. I was surrounded by the Virgin Mary, and even went to a high school named Marian. Yet I never felt any real spiritual juice there, much to the dismay of my rosary-spinning Irish Catholic grandmother. (She called me her lost sheep.) Even at a young age, I noticed that the priests, altar boys, and Cardinals were all men, wearing fancy dresses and performing rituals that lacked meaning for me. The incense made me faint. The women, lay helpers and nuns, dutifully did the altar dishes. I felt like an outsider, a weekly visitor. I was hungry for something more, though I was unable to name it.

This hunger in my Soul, and a series of challenging life events in my early twenties, led me on a search. I was depressed and confused about all the possibilities for my new post-college life and what I was supposed to make of it. I started a new job and met a friend while riding the commuter train to work in Boston. Donna had pixie-short hair, a bright smile and a twinkle in her eye. We struck up an easy friendship full of stimulating conversation, which opened up a whole new world to me.

Each week we avidly studied new books on meditation, metaphysics, and all kinds of spirituality. We got tarot and tea-leaf readings in seedy parts of Boston; we explored astrology and crystal healing workshops in New Age bookstores all over hip Cambridge. I found Lynn Andrews' *Medicine Woman* books and longed to have her magical adventures. Jealously, I wondered, "Why can't I be her and have that happen to me?" (Be careful what you ask for.) Little did I know that my own mystical journey was about to begin.

Perfect Plans

I worked for years as a commercial artist and fashion designer but I became weary of exploiting my creative gifts for corporate profit. I longed to immerse myself in pure unadulterated creative expression, and yet knew I needed a practical trade to make a living. One day, just weeks before enrolling in a Master of Fine Arts in Boston, I was riding the subway at rush hour. I recall looking at a grimy tile wall as the train screeched to a stop, when out of nowhere I heard, "Go study *Art Therapy*." I had never heard of this profession before, but the unexpected directive sure made me curious. Following this mysterious guidance, I immediately started my research. I quickly saw that this career could feed my creative, spiritual, social, and practical needs all at once. The perfection magnified when I discovered the ideal Master's degree program just four blocks from my apartment. I completely shifted plans and started within weeks. My adventure had begun.

Exploring Soul and Spirit

I didn't get direct Divine guidance like that very often, but my spiritual path continued as I dove into Expressive Arts Therapy. I started meditating and delving into the world of angels and spirit guides. Immersed in my investigation of creativity, healing, and Soul, I used journaling as a way to process my myriad thoughts, feelings and experiences. As I wrote, a curious thing started to happen. I discovered I could pray and ask a question about my situation and receive answers that helped. I could tap into a deeper part of myself and connect with higher wisdom and guidance. I found it incredibly soothing, supportive, and helpful. I started calling this guided writing meditation practice *Listening to Spirit* or just *Listening*, for short.

As part of my morning practices—those rituals of connection and self-care that I find critical for my own balance and well-being—I'd open a blank page in my journal (now a document on my laptop). After quieting my mind, tuning in to myself, and connecting to Spirit, I'd open up and ask questions about my life. I'd feel a gentle shift, like a cool, fragrant breeze and sense a response. Often, the guidance came from a group of angels who described themselves as my "Soul team."

Through time, I developed an attuned ear and body-sense for discerning what guidance was coming to me—choosing the exquisitely right phrases—versus what I wanted or would like to hear. Often, I've been surprised by the answers I've received. I've used this process when I face "big" issues, such as my life purpose or career questions. I also use it for smaller decisions, to determine whether they are Soul-congruent and purposeful: travel logistics, daily work flow, relationship conundrums, or business plans. When I do, I find my worry is soothed and my day moves with more ease, grace, joy, and synchronicity. *Listening* is practical mysticism for everyday life. Anyone who desires it can have this kind of spiritual connection, and it is immensely helpful.

Searching Deeper

Meanwhile, I began exploring Native American and Celtic shamanism, seeing that path of traveling into the Spirit world as parallel to journeying into the creative unconscious through Expressive Arts Therapy. Both are sacred expeditions into the archetypal depths of Soul. (I developed this theme in my Master's thesis on Shamanic Art Therapy.) I explored the Goddess through women's circles which were bursting on the post-feminist scene and spreading like wildfire. I loved the tangible, clear access—a through-line into the Spirit world. This sparked my curiosity about similar traditions and deeper mysteries in my own lineage.

I started to wonder: Where are the earth-based spiritual practices of my ancestors from Europe? Did Christianity have these direct-access methods, and why were they hidden teachings? My own upbringing didn't point to it, yet many other faiths seemed to have a mystical path: Islam has Sufism, Judaism the Kabbalah, and Taoism the Tao Te Ching. What were the esoteric teachings from my European lineage that offered direct connection to the God within?

Flame Ignites

The yearning of my Spirit was answered when I met a pivotal mentor who taught women's mysteries and the lost wisdom of the female fertility cycle through the lens of Esoteric Christianity. Tamara Slayton had a strong mystical connection to Mother Mary as Goddess, which sparked a new flame in me. Finally, I found a deeper perspective into the Divine that my heart and Soul could relate to—a deity who reflected my female form.

As I connected with the Madonna, I found Mary Magdalene profoundly compelling. I was drawn to the mysteries of Mary—Madonna and Magdalene, the mother and the priestess—as two sides of the same archetypal coin. Mary Magdalene's story was mysterious, veiled, and conflicted, captivating despite her infamy. She called to me like a beacon in a dark night of Soul.

I continued my spiritual practices in guided meditation, creative arts, and body-centered movement therapies as I developed my private practice, while living an easy, eclectic, country life on the West Coast. My Sister Circle met with the cycles of the moon for a decade, reweaving sacred, tattered threads of Feminine Soul by celebrating the beauty of our lives in artful rituals. My connection to Mary Magdalene remained a golden tether to my Soul, weaving in and out. I studied what I could, but in the pre-Internet days, Magdalene was not so easy to find. Often I felt without a community, ideology, practice, or home to ground these explorations. Nonetheless, I now see the destiny thread that pointed, nudged, and called me to this path of the Sacred Feminine.

Whispers of Destiny

Fast forward to 2007. I was living a good life in Oregon with a beautiful home, dear friends, loving relationship, financial stability, and enriching work with my clients, but something was amiss. I started feeling strong yearnings about finding my real reason for being here on this planet. I sensed that there were big shifts ahead, a deeper destiny that I was here to serve. I returned to my *Listening* practice for guidance about life decisions, direction, and other changes. I started getting guidance from Spirit, which started this book—glimmers about the awakening of the Divine Feminine like this:

"Notice that the theme you are awakening in yourself you can do so with others. Use the tools you have at your access for connecting with guides and inner wisdom. Share these with others. Awaken the Feminine Divine. Listen deeply from the heart of your Soul. Re-member your Soul purpose, your Divine destiny.

The Divine She is within you and speaks through you. The time is ripe. It is time we awaken the power that is inherent in the Beauty and Soul of the Feminine. The Divine in female form comes from silence as well as speaking, from listening to and living from a deep inner place that honors all life. This is not only for women to do, though women carry this and must lead."

Curious, I wondered where that would lead.

Recipe of Purpose

In retrospect, the various components of my journey add up to a perfect recipe for what unfolded as my purpose. Nonetheless, I was surprised. As you will read later, the guidance continued when Magdalene appeared to me in a vision. She encouraged me to write her perspective on the Sacred Feminine, with her story, skills, and practices. She expressed the importance of sharing this new body of work with other women to reclaim the Divine Feminine *now*.

So, on a weekly basis, I communed with Mary Magdalene, a greatly misunderstood woman of power, mystery, and wisdom. Using the practice of *Listening*, I would simply open my connection to her via prayer and meditation, hear (or sense) her voice, and write. Her communication to me (what I call *Divine Downloads*) resulted in many pages of journaling, which ultimately became this book.

At this point, you may be thinking that I'm crazy or that I have a rare gift. I am not sure either is the case. My experience of being with Mary Magdalene (or other guides) in meditation feels very ordinary and down-to-earth. I've taught hundreds of people how to navigate their life path by *Listening* to their intuitive source of wisdom and guidance. My hope is that by reading The Magdalene Path, you might realize (or find the courage to admit) that you have this ability, too. It's latent in all of us; we just need guidance and permission. I'm here to give you both. I love teaching this process to others. Should you be interested in trying this for yourself, go to the *Free Resources* section of my website, MagdalenePath.com, and download the activity "Listening to Spirit."

What follows are my regular (albeit unusual) dialogues with Mary Magdalene, who I've come to know as a brilliant teacher of light and love. She clarifies her conflicted role in history with stories of her life that we finally need to know. Perhaps even more important is her perspective about the awakening of Feminine Soul and the myriad ways it relates to our culture today. Her message is profound, passionate, and intensely relevant to our lives as women. Also included are skills, practices, and activities to put her teachings to use in your everyday life. I hope her words will move you as they have me—into a richer, deeper, juicier, more Soul-centered place in your life.

Compass Points of Bliss

By working with the teachings in this book, you can reconnect with your own radiant feminine vitality and brilliance. Yes! Using the practices that are woven into the chapters, you can (re)awaken your Soul path and radically improve your life—surrender your struggle with a life out of balance. I've culled out all the practices in the book into a separate, stand-alone workbook that you can refer back to, so you can make notes if you're borrowing the book from a friend or reading an e-book. You can download the workbook and other helpful resources by going to MagdalenePath.com.

The Magdalene Path is a life-altering recipe for grace, ease, flow, intuition, creativity, and sensuality—the compass points for bliss. The insights, perspectives, and tools within these pages are powerful and timely. The lessons that follow can transform you; as you change, so will the world around you. It is a big shift. Get ready.

Women have very distinct talents and gifts that are vital to the health of society and our planet right now. We are being called to lead in a new way that is uniquely feminine. A new path of empowerment, the Divine Feminine priestess, is emerging. Let the pages ahead unveil the great beauty of your Soul's creative essence and the rich gems within. Be prepared to sparkle!

Angel of Desire, © 2014 Claire Sierra

CHAPTER 1

Magdalene Messages

Divine Download

In the winter of 2007-2008, I'd been going through a spell of malaise—an old familiar funk that centered on feeling adrift in my life. I longed to know who I really was and what I came to be/do in this lifetime. From the outside, my life looked pretty good, but inside I knew there was more. I just couldn't figure out what that was. I had a gnawing sense that there was something I was supposed to be doing. It felt close, and yet it eluded me.

So I made a cup of tea and settled into my chair. I centered myself, through my morning meditation and prayers, to ask Spirit for guidance and direction about the coming year. I started by slowing my breath, attempting to still my busy mind for 20 minutes or so in order to connect with my inner being. My Spirit guidance team (angels, Divine beings and ancestors) came immediately, as they always do when I remember to use this practice. Speaking as a collective group, they encouraged me to go into the practice I call *Listening*. Here is what they shared:

Spirit: You have not yet stopped long enough to let us in. You may not yet understand the grace we offer you and how it will increase the ease of your work life. You work harder than you must because you are afraid to let go. There is more ease and flow available when you allow the Divine in to the planning and execution of your day. In other words, allow time and space for Spirit to be with you. A regular, even casual period of sitting, relaxing, and listening will benefit you immensely.

In deeper Listening, you can hear the suggestions that can allow you to manifest in a more physical, tangible way into the world. Be confident of your ability to receive guidance from us. Your fear itself serves as a strong block to the flow of your reception. As your overall resistance to Listening decreases, you will find greater success and enjoyment. The one called the Magdalene wishes to speak with you and share her wisdom and energy.

Mary Magdalene: Greetings, shining guardian of the mysteries, Keeper of Secrets of The Way. We (your Soul guidance team) delight in the recent interest in my story. It is the oldest tale of neglect and betrayal—centuries of denying my presence, accomplishment, and stature by those in power. This developed into a bigger wound to humanity than the loss of my personal "herstory." It resulted in a deep dishonoring and discounting of the feminine, experienced by all women for millennia. In this we misplaced the balance of power between Jesus the Christ and myself, The Magdalene. This was a magnificent and supreme experience—one we are coming back around to 2000 years later. This is a huge loss, for it has sorely upset the balance and dynamic between the masculine and feminine principles. But I am getting ahead of myself.

What I want to convey to you is my immense pleasure. Overjoyed I am at the opportunity to present myself to you. You have held onto the thread of the story throughout. It is becoming ever clearer to you why it might be important to do so. There is information that was damaged or seriously misconstrued that needs to be set right.

The fields of your culture will lay fallow and barren while the Goddess bride is cast out of the Divine marriage. The Holy Pair is torn apart. The bridegroom, the Christian's male God, can only hold his half. The effect is apparent in your land—in spite of "expert" testimony to the contrary. Life is uneven and out of balance. It is no longer working. It is far easier and more convenient to be in denial. There is work to be done in bringing balance back to the masculine and feminine. Harmony is in the process of being restored.

Your part is to sit and listen, to receive and convey. Trust the process; it will reveal itself as it unfolds. I have waited a long time for this moment, for this return to my rightful place in the understanding of humanity. Not for my ego's sake, though yes, it is hard to endure 2000 years (two millennia), of misunderstanding, soiled reputation, and general "bad publicity." I was never a whore, nor did I have devils within me. I was a priestess, healer and leader, which was far more dangerous, to some. More on that in a moment.

I come now for the truth to become known and for the story of Christ to be lived. Worship of one man was never the intention. It is a turn in the path. He was like God, of God, but that does not mean he is God, any more than you or I. But we are jumping ahead to a tale for another day.

I felt uplifted by this transmission. I was relieved and delighted to get some direction, and yet anxieties filled my busy mind. What if, this and that. I thought, "Is this really happening to me?" I knew I wasn't making it up. The guidance I heard felt clear and accurate. (And I certainly wouldn't have thought of those things on my own.) I wondered if I could carry out her direction. I had concerns about my ability to do this "life purpose project," I wasn't an expert. I worried about whether I'd have anything new to add to what's been written about Mary Magdalene or the Divine Feminine. Yet the urging was consistent. I only knew one thing: I was supposed to pray, connect, and write.

At moments I embraced her guidance, but just as often I got distracted by my own fears and concerns. Somehow I was supposed to imbue this knowledge so that I could awaken the world to the presence of the Divine Feminine? That seemed like a tall order, but I was intrigued and curious.

Sacred Contract

A week or so passed. The busyness and business of life was getting in the way. I sensed that I needed to make time to sit and allow Mary Magdalene to come to me again. So I made a cup of jasmine green tea, steeping while I completed my brief morning practice. I started with meditation, finding a spot in my house that had as much light as I could find in this dark time of year. When I finally settled into my vintage chartreuse couch, I felt a gentle nudge; the presence of Magdalene beckoned my attention. I grabbed my computer, so I could capture what she wanted to share with me that day. This is the message I received:

Mary Magdalene: Blessings dear one, it is with great anticipation that we come to you again. We say "we" because we are a group collection of consciousness and our energy is large and uncontained. "I" sounds so finite and in human terms, small. The presence we carry, which you now feel, is vast. Yes, we are the energy that embodies Mary the Magdalene.

Claire: It is confusing to me. I experience you as the individualized essence of Mary Magdalene. Is that incorrect?

Mary Magdalene: No, but I speak on behalf of many who are your guides. I am not only speaking for myself, because my consciousness is expanded beyond the individual expression of Self. That is what I am saying.

Also, you must recall the Divine pairing of Bride and Beloved. I stand with my beloved, Yeshua, and although you do not relate to him much, he is here.

Claire: Yeshua. You mean Jesus (as we know him)?

Mary Magdalene: Who else? Of course, yes.

Claire: So, you are speaking as an expanded consciousness, as the couple, as my group of guides, and as the collective of Magdalenes?

Mary Magdalene: No, you are mistaken. The collective are the Mari, the priestesses. I will explain more about them later. You are a Magdalene, meaning that you carry the spiritual lineage of leadership, but the Priestesses of Magdalene were not all Magdalenes. Only the High Priestess was The Magdalene.

Claire: Oh, that's interesting. That is a lot of people to be speaking for.

Mary Magdalene: Yes, so now you understand. I do sometimes speak for myself as I, but it is like when you speak to friends, you sometime speak for yourself as "I," sometimes for you and your mate or your team or family as "we." There are many positions you can speak from and no one doubts your individuality. That is how you shall hold me, and us.

Claire: Okay, that makes sense now. Is there more you wish to share today?

Mary Magdalene: We are so happy that there is such interest in the Truth of my Divine Union with the Christ. It is time for this knowledge to be shared. There is so much to say it is hard to know where to begin.

We are grateful that you are willing and request your patience if these messages seem long-winded and meandering. It is certainly not our intention. Our intention, if we are so bold, is to channel the teachings from the one called Magdalene, through you, to the world. We felt the deep hungering in the Earth for the Divine Feminine. While I, Mary Magdalene, am not the only path, I am the partner/consort lost from the Christian teaching that is so dominant in the mindfield of your culture.

Our desire is to share what was lost when the sacred marriage was dropped from the Christian story of The Bible. With that, the blessings of the Sacred Feminine through the Magdalene were also lost. There are lessons and tools that are part of the Magdalene Path that we would like to impart to the world (or those interested) through you.

We believe you are well suited due to your interest, willingness, and desire. This does not make you special. This humility is important as it can be easy to think one has special traits or characteristics that allow others (or self) to hold one above the rest.

However, these are ways you have practiced or are cultivating and thus are in alignment with. Again, this does not make you better or more special. You are willing, practiced, and available. You have been waiting "on assignment" for a long time: generations of life experience or incarnations. Your Soul knows this sacred contract. We are very grateful that this is coming to fruition.

The Path of the Magdalene is a large topic on this short evening. You've wanted an outline to guide you, so here it is. We see this broken up into 8 parts, chapters:

1. Context – A brief history and overview of your experience, how you have come to see the role of Mary Magdalene, as an overview/review of what has been opened and so aptly explored by others. A review of the territory, if you will.

2. Magdalene's Story - My "herstory", which may differ from what the others believe, my Temple upbringing and training, which impacted the life of Jesus, the Christed one.

3-7. *The Magdalene Path, A.K.A. The Way of Light and Love – Specific practices for bringing in and holding energy, including activities and "home study" practices.*

8. Review/Conclusion/Closure

Magdalene's message impacted me profoundly. Having a blueprint like this soothed me immensely. The directness and specificity left me speechless. It appeared that I was being called into a sacred contract that my Soul prepared for. I found myself reeling for a few days, as I digested this. Yet I also felt excited and inspired.

Entering the Temple

I knew I "should" be connecting with Mary Magdalene in my meditations and writing and take up this Soul contract, but I stumbled for a few weeks before following through. It's awkward to admit, since the guidance was so clear and it obviously was a direct answer to my prayers and pleading for more information about my Divine purpose. For some reason, I just couldn't get myself there and instead used all my best strategies of distraction, avoidance, and denial.

After dancing around it, I finally sat still for my *Listening* practice. Quieting my mind in meditation, I prayed and opened to the light and energy of Mary Magdalene. I was grateful that she arrived within moments, despite my ambivalence. This surprised me, but as she shared her story, I learned she was not going to let me stumble.

Claire: It seems I am remiss in coming here to speak to you more. I feel blocked somehow. I notice I get distracted and I'm procrastinating. I imagine this is resistance or fear, but why or to what I do not know.

Mary Magdalene: We think you are not ready or are afraid of the bigness of what might occur. This sends out a block and we are not able to transmit through this interference. We also sense your excitement and anticipation, which too can create blocks because you are expecting something "big" to happen. We are patient and willing to wait. Let us start with a story of my time in the Temple, when I was a young girl.

At first I could not believe all that was happening to me. I had grown up in a small village and my life was full of wealth and luxury. I could not imagine that at such a young age I would be leaving home. I knew this was my plan, my path, but I hardly felt ready. And it was my tenth birthday, of all days!

Many of the young girls from privileged families were sent to the Temple for education and training. Some were limited in what they were allowed to learn. I was pleased there were no restrictions placed upon me, as my father, the head of our household by any definition of our time, was open-minded about the education of girl children. Some girls were denied book-learning, while I already knew how to read. Others were denied the arts of the Temple priestesses, as there were growing beliefs that this conflicted with our Jewish heritage and practices.

Luckily for me, my father, held none of these constraints. He was a strong man, a provincial leader and prominent businessman (by your understanding today). He was confident that nothing I could learn would take me from my roots, our heritage. He was right in some ways, and wrong in others. But that had more to do with my destiny than anything he held sway over.

My father was in a sense a prince or lord, which made me a princess. There is nothing we did without. We lived in a lavish home, with carpets, fine furnishings, lanterns, servants, and all manner of luxury by the standards of our day and culture. I was the eldest daughter. I had a younger sister and brother. My brother followed after my father into the world. I did not know much of him and his upbringing, as he was a small child when I left home to study at the Temple.

The Magdalene Path

When I arrived at the Temple there was great fanfare. It was important and foretold by the Temple oracle that a daughter from the house of Benjamin would arrive when I did. My arrival was the fulfillment of prophesy and also brought a great financial boon. It also signaled an acceptance of their ways in a time when these beliefs and practices were becoming uncertain.

The Temple had been there for as long as anyone could remember, dating far back in time. Yet the Jewish faith, of which we were part, was changing. The ways of the Temple priestesses wove different beliefs that were not always in agreement with the Jewish practices that were becoming more common. Our knowledge and practices were becoming forbidden ground. We were moving farther and farther away from the Goddess and the partnership that had always been held as sacred between God almighty and his powerful Goddess consort.

So as a young Jewess to go to the Temple was a great honor and privilege, yet also a great mystery. Why was it so forbidden? Surely, there were rumors about serpent worship, sex magic, idol worship, and other things, but all of these were whispers at the well. I had seen the priestesses of Isis and others in the marketplace, and they always held themselves with such decorum; certainly, they didn't seem unclean or unholy to me at all. In fact, just the opposite—their power and mystery was palpable. Of course, I was a young girl, what did I know? To me they were very exotic and glamorous.

At the time of my entry to the Temple I was sad to leave my family home, but I thought, living nearby I would see them often. I would stay a few years and after my education was complete return home to marriage. I'd move into my husband's family home, as was custom at the time. There was rumor, whisperings among the mothers, of my destiny with the heir of David. But I tried to avoid thinking about the young Yeshua. We had known each other all of our lives. I could hardly fathom all their talk of uniting kingdoms and saving the people. That entire fate seemed too far-fetched for me.

After getting this guidance, I read it several times. I was moved by the potent clarity of what Mary Magdalene relayed in this piece of writing that flew through my fingers. On one level, I felt totally awestruck. So much of this was beyond the scope of my knowledge. And yet paradoxically, it felt so normal, so non-extraordinary to be happening at all.

Mass Movement of Peace

A week or so passed. After receiving the last Divine Download, I put it aside, almost forgetting about it, and went on with a very busy, mundane life. At some point, I re-read the passage about the Temple and was again so stirred by the magic and mystery that it conveyed. I recognized that I still avoided diving into this meditation/writing project. My life also provided excellent distraction, in spite of my quest for higher purpose. I was busy with my work, husband, social life, and volunteer projects in my community. But still… an amazing thing was available to me, and I was hesitating. I felt sheepish and perplexed.

I finally got myself to sit and close my eyes. I slowed my breath and drew in the light. My body, mind, and spirit all started to pool and settle. I relaxed and surrendered. Inwardly, I reached out and called Mary Magdalene. She appeared immediately. I didn't see her physically, but in my mind's eye I sensed her presence: strong, gentle, clear, and vibrant. Whole and holy. My disquiet was immediately addressed as our conversation began.

Mary Magdalene: Greetings, dear one. We are happy to be with you again. We do not despair the time in between our meetings, and you should not as well. That feeling of remorse or guilt is not going to help the process flow. Release your misgivings about "not doing it right" or more frequently. We are solely interested that this information be conveyed to you, then you may do with it as you wish.

So for today, please dispense with the ruminations of lack that are penetrating your mind field. We are full of joy at this opportunity coming to pass during this time on your planet, when the true comprehension of the Christ people can be realized. The truth is so close to you every day, but because of training from your culture, you do not see it.

There are many forces at play now to counteract this. There is a mass movement in the consciousness of the Earth toward peace, justice, and truth. At the core of this is the misconstrued, misunderstood knowledge of the Christ called Jesus and his companions, the disciples or apostles. Certainly, the misinformation about his marriage partnership and children with me, Mary Magdalene, is a grave error that could not have been foreseen 2000 years ago.

Now your culture is so close to collapse under the imbalance of the feminine and masculine archetypes. That weight is about to tumble. It is of utmost importance that you understand we are not talking about societal collapse, for that knowledge would generate fear and turmoil all its own.

We are talking about a reweaving of understanding. While that might make things topsy-turvy for some time, it will not stimulate full-scale economic or political collapse. Now certainly, events are not fore-written, so things could evolve differently and go awry. But that is not the likely scenario we see, with all the changes happening in human consciousness. We see all beings desiring peace, harmony, and Oneness aligned with gratitude, abundance, and the law of attraction.

Certainly, there will be outrage and anger. The intermingling of religious/ political power structure (especially as it relates to royalty) will be challenged. Justice will be called for. For certain individuals and in some societies, this new knowledge could be devastating. It all depends on how the people decide to take it and what they choose do with it. It can bring tremendous freedom and joy. All these events are intertwined to make a stable basket into which change will take place.

So we are delighted at your interest and study in the fulfillment of purpose. We are especially proud of your willingness to confront dominant thoughtfields that create oppression in the minds and hearts of humans in your world. We are very aware of how ideas and beliefs about things like prosperity, gratitude, and abundance affect how you see and respond to the world.

We are here to tell you that you are on the right path and not to deter for fears of "wasting time." You are wasting not a second. You are doing exactly as your Soul intended, and it is with great joy we let you know that this time you have is here for these reasons. Right now.

This awareness that you are gaining is furthering you on the Magdalene Path. This knowing was part of the original teaching of the Christ couple. Both of us brought powerful energy to the pair. In losing the female perspective, the world only got half the wisdom. Even that became distorted, as it became all about him—a man who was turned into a God.

Christ as Jesus (who we called Yeshua, Easa, and later Jhesis — many names, same man) never intended to turn into a God. That was not our plan or intent. But we did not know how the story would play out either. We knew his methods and teachings were a challenge to the common culture, an occupied land. But the minds of men took our story and gave it a spin that would serve their own needs. Even that was not so sinister originally, though it was not totally naïve either.

Early members of what became the Christian church did not foresee the huge political monolith that the church authority would become. Remember, these men and women were the minority at the time, regularly rounded up and killed for their beliefs. They did, however, understand how their teaching had to be conveyed in cultures that still worshipped gods. And thus the information evolved to match that common understanding.

There have always been others who opposed the doctrine that turned Jesus into a God. That lineage is hidden today. That has become a quieter tale, not so evident in common religious paradigms that have emerged today.

What has evolved through time was not originally part of a conspiracy to negate the feminine. Though the individual players—the apostles and their followers—did spin the story into their own web and their motives were not always pure. Some errors were sheer accident, matters of linguistic and cultural translation, reframed 2000 years hence. Other versions were the makings of politico-religious leaders, generations or centuries later. From the context of your now, with religion and politics separated—ideologically at least—this is a challenge to recognize. Understand that, for many centuries, this was not the case. Religious leaders held much sway in the workings of royalty and leadership.

We are not here to name names and make accusations. It seems pointless and obvious. Name-calling will not help the situation, only creating more arguments and divisions among those who like to think of themselves as learned scholars of scripture. We instead would like to focus on the parts of the story that have not been told, or not told in entirety. The rest will fall into place.

This encouragement felt beautiful and exciting. I was amazed at the fluidity of what I was hearing in meditation—the unusual yet specific grammar and vocabulary as well as the insights that came forth. I was inspired and intrigued, yet again.

Discern Your Truth

I started getting into a flow, and I came more eagerly to my next session, curious about what would transpire. I had no idea how this story was to be told, but that seemed to be part of this process: to surrender. I felt grateful and eager, if not a bit bewildered by it all. I noticed that after I reviewed the previous Divine Download, my inspiration and motivation rose, but so did my doubts and fears. These worries were the source of my avoidance/resistance and could derail me, so I focused on letting them go and being present.

Mary Magdalene: Thank you for welcoming me into your heart and mind for so long. It is such a joy and relief to have this opportunity to speak with you and through you. Yes, it is really me and you must dispense with the doubting thoughts and comparisons to others. Fear not the accusations of falsehood by others. Their niggling is not yours to be concerned about. You are the barometer for your own truth.

This is my first lesson for you: Discern your own Truth. *What are the ways in which we discern Truth? We look to the mind and the body. Each has great tools to help in this process. First, by being honest with ourselves about the motives we might have to believe something. Remember that a belief is nothing other than a concept or idea, thought over and over. It is through repetition in one's own mind, or one's family or cultural mind that a thought becomes an idea, which becomes a belief.*

Yes, you have different layers of mind, from the personal to the universal. Carl Jung developed this as the concept of the collective unconscious. Your beliefs are fluid, as your thoughts are fluid. There is great freedom here. However, you are taught as young children that beliefs are solid, like concrete. This is not so. They are passed to you by your culture, family, friends, and media. These ideas are everywhere and they become embedded into the mindfield.

When you are born you "log in" to that mindfield and have access to all those beliefs that reflect your heritage, culture, class, religion, gender, family story, etc. It is general and specific. You tend to gather yourselves together, living and socializing according to similarities, for comfort and safety. "Birds of a feather flock together," is an example of this. You actually have great freedom, however, and you are now learning, as a species, that you can change your beliefs. For some this is great freedom. For others, this causes great anxiety and confusion, as they fear not knowing what to choose. They have been taught to mistrust themselves and to go to another for answers or guidance. This worked well for those in power, either religious or political.

Choose Your Beliefs

So there is safety in the choice not to choose. Some decide to remain ignorant of the ability to change one's mind. For others, there is great freedom to change some beliefs, but not others. Some are held more rigidly—as facts, not beliefs. We see the environment and money as two areas that people love to get rigid and fixed about. Again, these attitudes are changing. As there is movement in the population toward more flexible beliefs, then there will be more mobility around entrenched, solid thoughtfields, such as what is happening in the physical domain of your Earth.

It important that you realize that your beliefs are whatever you choose them to be. It is really that simple. There are others who will argue that with you. That is fear (yours as well as theirs), serving to keep you small and afraid. It is harder to shift a belief when others you respect are arguing against the change you wish to see.

Nonetheless, you are able to shift what you see and what you believe. This is a function of focus. Whatever you give your attention to will shine. You will see/hear/experience more of it and it will grow. In growing, you will see/hear/experience further and the cycle will continue. This can go toward the good or the bad. You choose which direction you want.

Law of Attraction

Naturally, there are those who will find exceptions to this. Yet their exceptions are often more about someone not wanting to believe and take responsibility for their own experience. This can be so painful. This is a Divine Law, the Law of Attraction. Are there exceptions to the Law of Gravity?

Often, the exceptions that are not blame-shifting are Divine intervention, Soul contracts, unconscious motivations, silent unspoken prayers, or other alternative realities one doesn't readily admit to. As you realize these new truths that are emerging right before your eyes, take care not to be harsh, blameful, and regretful about your past events. One must have patience, faith, and compassion, *for oneself and others.*

Remember to have compassion *for yourself about what you did not know, as one would not blame a child for not knowing the alphabet or how to tie shoes. Have* patience, *for as you learn, you still slip and regress, forgetting you inherently have the power and possibility of creating the life you desire. Have* patience *as it takes time to acclimate and retool your mental patterns to accommodate these new awarenesses.*

For some, it is like a bolt of lightning that hits and shifts one's consciousness completely and entirely. But for most it is a gradual process of easing in as you practice—remembering, forgetting, and remembering again—each time connecting longer and more fully with what you are capable of.

Cultivate faith *that you know this as Truth under Divine Law, your birthright. Have* faith *that there is a larger force out there (and in there). It is guiding, protecting, and encouraging this new awareness that is awakening for the human family. This is a planetary evolution that links to the larger galactic community and the universal whole.*

You are not alone. When you all recognize that the learning and growing you each do is not for you alone, things will get easier. There is help available, always. You need simply to reach out in your awareness and ask. But this is another lesson, and for today we shall leave it as that.

Teachers of Possibility

When the Christed One (Yeshua, your Jesus) and the Magdalene walked on this plane, our gift was to teach people of possibilities. We understood, through our own talent and training, that humans were infinitely more than all have been led to believe. Our gift and goal was to teach that to everyone.

When Yeshua said "do this in memory of me," or "The Magdalene's name will be remembered always," or "I do this to show you that you can do this and more," we meant this literally. We were not showing how great he was and how he should be worshipped. Christ coming to Earth was never meant to be about worship of him. Surely a teacher can be honored and respected, but two millennia of thinking a gifted man is a God insults all of humanity and your own greatness as beings of light.

Do you see how that implication of his Godhood serves the leaders and diminishes the followers? How can you ever progress and practice the "miracles" we showed you all how to do, if you believe he is special and you are just meant to follow along for the ride? Your "salvation" is from riding his coattails with adornment and worship.

That is not the teaching we imparted. We are returning now to share how the energy can be received, and how miracles are performed. You all have this ability. This was always our prime teaching: God/Goddess is within each of you, ready to pour out into your world.

We never intended to disempower you of your birthright. Our coming into a historically rigid religious culture made for a more challenging receipt of the message. The Law—traditional Judaism—in that first century was strict, and there were many obstacles in the everyday that are not so apparent now. We are most pleased to see the interest in the truth of our ministry, though we recognize you are bucking a current that is 2000-plus years in the making.

It is not a new story, and it is harder to tell an old story anew. There are so many pictures and "truths" that are already in place and assumed to be historically accurate (when they are not). These need to be dismantled and removed. But help is on the way, and we feel it is time and you are ripe. We can add more about beliefs, but feel for now we have covered the topic adequately.

I was really inspired by this powerful download. As I explored my own attitudes and core beliefs, beautiful changes occurred in me. Then I quickly lost track of the amazing bounty and went on with my life, as if nothing was happening. I wondered how often others got amazing insights or information and then conveniently forgot. I also pondered whether that would be part of the message modeled in this book.

Infusion of Magic and Mystery

As I attempted to get into a rhythm for this project, I struggled with focus and integrating Magdalene's wisdom into my daily life. When I reviewed her guidance, I got inspired, but it didn't stick for long. So when I centered for meditation for this day, Magdalene came immediately and coached me in the kindest, yet clearest manner.

Mary Magdalene: Today we have a story for you. This story is about you, though. We would like you to recall that time in retreat in the Berkshire Mountains of Massachusetts. You were in your late 20s, at a Full Moon ceremony with a circle of women—modern day priestesses in a sacred grove.

During meditation, the moon came down and carried you away for a time and blessed you. She spoke to you and bestowed on you the mantle of Magdalena, a name you have carried ever since.

Claire: Yes. I remember it clearly, still. It was Beltane (the Celtic holiday of spring rebirth and renewal on the first of May), I believe.

Mary Magdalene: Recall that you were in a circle of sister-friends, some you knew and others you did not, during a time in your life that was filled with lots of prayer, meditation, and ceremony with women. You felt safe, loved, pure, and alive. When the moon came to you and named you, you knew this was real. It was as real an event as anything you have ever experienced, right?

Claire: Yes.

Mary Magdalene: You discerned your own Truth. And yet to many this could be make-believe, meaning fictional or imaginary. Yet that was your initiation into our circle. So this is how we would like this work we are doing to be: fiction or make-believe, and yet very, very real.

Make-believe is a way of being (usually through play or story) that makes up new stories and beliefs over old ones. We would like this process with you to be infused with magic and mystery that invokes a certain experience of time and place — in this world yet not of it. To make you believe.

Claire: That sounds fascinating and fabulous. I don't know how to do that.

Mary Magdalene: Let go: let us be the driver, you be the car. Surrender, my dear, let us show you The Way.

This was surprising, to be taught with a story from my own past, which I had all but forgotten about. It was disconcerting and befuddling at first. Yet I evaluated that event in a new and deeper way. I really saw what Magdalene was trying to show me. It was beautiful to behold. My life was magical and I was having incredible experiences when I could allow them in. I just couldn't see it because my perceptions, fears, and judgments blocked me. My spiritual experiences felt natural when they occurred, not outrageous like they are someone else's book or movie. I realized that I needed to put fewer boxes around my adventures, or I ran the risk of missing them entirely.

Shifting Consciousness

Each time I sat in *Listening* meditation, I never knew what would come through. That was obviously the design of the experience, since it kept my judging, controlling, analytical mind out. So I decided one morning to take Magdalene's advice to heart: to open up more and see what would happen.

Mary Magdalene: Believe (in yourself) and let go…..There was a time on your planet when all was a garden of delight (garden of the light, get it?) Some call that Eden, others call it Atlantis, Shangri-La, Valhalla — all these are names for this same magical place/time. Avalon was a part of that, too, though what you know of was later, when time was moving differently, consciousness was shifting, and the passages were fading.

That time and place still exists, but your awareness of it does not, because you do not know how to access it. What if you were able to experience those portals and visit those alternative realities? They are not different times as much as different planes of the same consciousness.

Consciousness is not actually the same now. The planes of reality are like different floors on a multi-story building. There are ways to access the floors. Think of it as you would stairs, or elevators. If you are not on that floor, you do not have access to the experience of being on that floor. You may see from the elevator a listing of the floor numbers, so you know they exist. But unless you press that button the elevator does not take you there, so you do not see into and experience that level of existence.

And so it is with reality. There are differing levels of consciousness that we may know exist. (Or may not; some are asleep to this.) You have access, but until you go there, you do not have any real experience of it. You may have awareness of it, but can only speculate, based on hypothesis, about the nature of the reality that exists there.

Humans do this all the time, as you project from the basis of your vision, experience, and so-called reality into the experience of another. You make assumptions about another person and choices made in their reality based on the observations from yours.

While this is hardly time-travel or inter-dimensional travel, it is an obvious way in which you shift from where you are into where you imagine someone else to be. It is quite commonplace to do so. We see that it is easy to misinterpret the version of reality another must be living, based on the position you view from.

We advise against it, though we know it is a challenging habit to break, and one that requires time and attention to do so. This is a mighty chunk to take on, and perhaps here we best stop for now.

From this passage, I was reminded that that our view of reality was really based from perception, and therefore to refrain from assessing someone else's choices from my limited vantage point. Magdalene was advising me to be more open, so that more levels of reality would unlock and different experiences would be available that were previously inaccessible. That seemed pretty awesome.

Soul Truth Prevails

These Divine Downloads via meditation were becoming really interesting. I was getting better at balancing this inner work with all my other (outer) obligations. I was doing my morning meditations most days. I badgered myself about it (though less) on the others. My lingering concern seemed centered on how others would perceive the message. I'm not a biblical scholar or a historian, and I worried that this might be *really* different than what writers I've loved and respected have written. What if people think I'm a kook for writing about this? Will I be able to bear that critique?

I decided to bring this to my meditation. I went upstairs to the alcove in my bedroom, deep in the evening. I settled into my brown stuffed chair, with a soft throw around my feet. Warmed by the quiet glow of a gentle light, I closed my eyes, softened my breath, and drew my attention inward. Again, I got encouragement and reassurance from Magdalene:

Mary Magdalene: As always, we are happy to commune with you. Despite obstacles we are in delight/the light. (We love that pun.) Be well. Please enjoy the wellness that you are. There is so much love and trust here of your beauty that you have no idea. We wish only the best and the brightest for you. We are hoping to reveal that to you in whatever timeframe you are willing to let us in. There is so much love for you, you have no imagination of. We are delighted, as always, that you would choose to spend any time with us, given the demands and attractions of your external world.

There is so much available about "Mary Magdalene" and that time in history that one can be overwhelmed in the search for Truth. Let us tell you that, while the study of the works of another can be of value, you must always be searching for the truth and the answer within. For it is with you that the answer to the Truth and questions of your Soul arrive. We are merely the messengers of those on high. You yourself know Truth. So the external path of study can be a folly, distraction.

It is distraction because it is a way of focusing outside of what is flowing within you. For within you is a fountain flowing supreme! It is a deep and potent well of creativity and inspiration. Yes, inside you. What you will find is amazing, so close and yet so far away for so many living in your time frame. There is so much distraction and entertainment.

Divine Authentic Presence

The Divine Truth flows to and through you. This guidance is worth acting on. You can learn to trust as you organize your life around it. This is where the priests and religious leaders of old became so nervous, for in directly accessing Source, all kinds of spiritual forces can be accessed. They did not trust people to have the discernment between good from bad and that your inherent choice would be for good. They did not trust you to know the difference. In other words, they worried that humans would choose evil, to channel the dark forces like their devil.

These men also bore concern that, without their guidance and intervention, their position of authority would be lost, fearing for their political and social position. Connection, direct access to Source, was discouraged and applied throughout orthodox teachings "for your own good." This theology is still evident today. Those with access to Spirit who were not part of their power structure were often killed or banished from society. Some were later martyred as saints, curiously enough.

Yet now we are in different times. Despite all of this, there is an increasing awareness that there is something grander looming ahead. You sense something for yourselves to be ready for, a bigger way to relate to reality, a great idea to open up to individually.

This is something that will make little sense to some, but that is okay. It is written for those that are waiting to hear and to know that it is time. Now is the time for the eternal up-leveling of Divine human-Spirit interaction. This is the date to bring in the Spirit that is eternally and unimaginably there.

As I pondered what "this time we are in" meant, and with whom this "up-leveling" was to occur. I sensed that this is indeed it, the time is now. And if not now, when? Who are we waiting for? What that means as a collective, cultural body is so different from what that means as an individual. This is where each of us is so vastly different.

It seems like we are waiting for a group event or for someone else to take charge. In fact, this change is something that comes from within each of us. In our own unique individuality, from the perspective of being in our authentic Truth, we each are called to do exactly what is congruent to us. No waiting or pretending any more.

We are living in a time, of all times, that requests our Divine authentic presence. Ultimately, each of us decides what that means. I was still getting clear on what it was for me, as this conversation and process unfolded.

Mary Magdalene: The denial of True Self never wins. The Soul always prevails, because it is the dominant vibration — the Truth of your unique Being, separate from the needs of the personality, the ego. It carries the day and trumps all other hands. Know that, in love and trust, we are delighted to be with you and encourage you. We look forward to this again.

Fallow

Despite the movement forward, this process came to a halt. I would have expected that, after crying out for guidance about my purpose and receiving this lucid and abundant text in response, I would have forged ahead. But my quest for Soul purpose sparked questions that required big life changes. I left my job, started a new career, opened and closed a new business, got married, and moved to a new city. Perhaps my worry and concerns hindered progress as well. Instead, I became immersed in the details of reconfiguring my life to meet a new calling that had not yet fully emerged.

I see this often with women on a Spirit path. We get on purpose, then we get off (or it looks like we are off), then we get on again. We might go to school or take a job and then have a baby, change jobs or tend a dying relative.[1] Each turn is more aligned and timely. A straight path becomes crooked and then straight again. Not so surprisingly, with all this outer movement and change, this inner project laid fallow for the next two years. My *Listening* practice remained active, providing guidance and support through the twists and turns that were a natural (but challenging) part of big life transitions. My work with Magdalene and the Divine Feminine was quiet, working in the background of my life.

---

1   Not that any of these activities is inherently on or off purpose – those choices are personal to your soul – but are given as examples of course correction. What is purposeful for one woman is not necessarily true for another. Choose wisely.

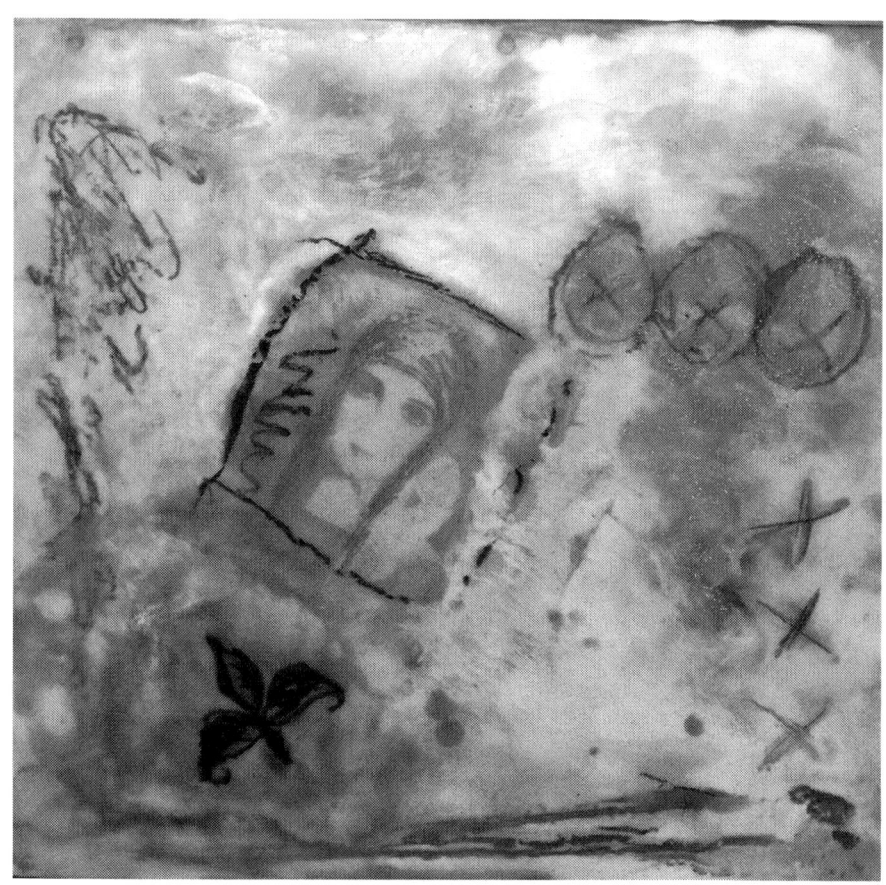

Hidden Mystery, © 2014 Claire Sierra

Chapter 2

Herstory

Magdalene Messages, Take Two

Fast forward, two years later. During autumn of 2009, the time, temperature, and conditions were ripe for my connection with Magdalene to become reestablished and flourish. As I was hungering for direction about my destiny path, big shifts occurred. I moved from my home of 16 years into a new community — a big change from a small, rural, hippy village. My husband and I bought a house in town and started a whole new life. I became absorbed in rebuilding my counseling and coaching practice, using art and creativity to help others shift from their misery to live a joyful, authentic life of their own design. I was barely settled into this new reality when my own quest for purpose started to churn again.

This yearning was answered when I got advanced professional training to help others find and live their life purpose. I refined my *Listening* practice, and got clearer access to my inner source of guidance, so that I trusted my experience more. Through my dialogue with Spirit, I learned about my purpose and addressed my fears and inner resistance.

As I guided others with this process, I started to be led me in another direction. During my *Listening* meditations, Divine guidance encouraged me to stop taking any more clients and put my art therapy/coaching practice aside. At first, I resisted this intensely. After all, I thought I had finally found my purpose. It was my passion as well as my livelihood. Instead, I was told over and over to "write and focus on the awakening of the Divine Feminine." Mary Magdalene came to me again, a remarkable encounter that I was forever changed by.

It was a glorious autumn afternoon: crisp, clear, and golden. I was lying on a massage table at my monthly acupuncture appointment. I loved this special room with the treatment table aligned under a large cathedral window. I relaxed as light streamed in from the south and warmed my body. Flute music played gently and relaxed me even more deeply. I entered meditation, as I often did there. My favorite meditation practice was to visualize light running through my body. Light flowed in from the crown of my head and out my feet, channeled by my breath. I felt tension and physical dis-ease flow out of me. I was infused with light—nourishment from the heavens—which felt rejuvenating and aligning.

As I did this, I entered a deeper layer of peace inside myself. The light started to become bigger, star-clustered, and brighter than the sunbeam coming in from outside. (I opened my eyes and peeked, just to be sure.) The room became charged, yet still. I became aware of a presence, a being of light, and Mary Magdalene started to speak. This soothed as well as surprised me. She shared that she wanted to tell me her story, her message and her tools of healing for the important task of unveiling the Divine Feminine. Lovingly, she encouraged me to do this project with her. I was in awe as I tried to absorb this immense experience.

After my acupuncture session ended, I tried to retain as much as I could remember while the experience was still fresh. I ran the images and ideas through my mind and quickly put pen to paper, scribbling to capture the essence of her transmission. I felt compelled, almost manic, because I knew how quickly these potent spiritual experiences faded—so indelibly clear one moment and gone the next, like water into sand. I raced home on my bike to reconstruct what I could from my notes and memory. As I did so, the dialogue process continued. She repeated everything, some of it from our earlier "forgotten" conversations, and we started the journey again.

Mary Magdalene: Greetings, dear one. As you have written, I am the one known as the Magdalene. I am one of many Priestesses of Light and I come to share the wisdom gifts of my teachings. There are tools that I will share that you may share with others. There are others that are meant for you to use and practice alone, sharing later once you have mastery. Today let me refresh your memory as we start our conversation anew.

Much has been written about me: much truth, much malice. There is no point finding fault, but it is no surprise that there are many who are interested in my life, for there is much to be gleaned. I carry a flame that cannot be extinguished. I am one in a long lineage of healers: women of power and mystery, wise-women, and priestesses. Through the centuries we have not always been favored and many among us have come to an early demise. I did not, though living in exile in a foreign land, my notoriety and influence was far different than had I stayed in the land of my birth.

As some have correctly suggested, I am from a royal family, one of the 12 Tribes of Israel, and on the priestess path. Most scholars are aware that the family line of Benjamin, from which I descend, was of the priestly clan. What is forgotten or swept away is that there was also a line of female priests and monks, who you would call priestesses, sisters, and nuns.

This is how I came to be a Mary. (Spelled "Mari" and pronounced "mahree." Notice the French pronunciation, Marie, is closest.) The name Mary is not a name at all. It is a title, much as today you could call someone "Mrs.," "Judge," or "Reverend."

Temple of Delight

As I mentioned before, I began training into the path of mystery of the God/Goddess, at an early age. In our time however, this was completely normal and it is a shame that the ensuing culture chose to wipe out that knowledge completely.

Nonetheless, in the time we lived, there were still temples devoted to the Goddess, as there were temples devoted to the God. There were temples that venerated both, and this was where I found myself. The training was still separate, as each gender, which are different energies, needs to cultivate its own power for the magic (the effect of your intention) to be effective. The practice of gender separation is often misunderstood in your time and land. It has been used as a means to split, discredit and dis-empower women. But in ours, this was well understood.

Women spent time in the temple devoted to the Goddess, the Sacred Feminine form of the all-creative universal Source. Men devoted time in their temple, which we will not spend much time discussing. The remnants are written about elsewhere and still in great evidence today.

The Temple we shared was a delight. The building was made of earth: rounded, smooth, and golden like the sun. Its thick walls kept us cool in hot weather and warm from fire in the cooler times. Benches were carved out of the walls with gemstones embedded in the cornices and around the windows. By the light of candles and oil lamps, the stones shimmered and sparkled with radiant light. Around the perimeter were hand-molded niches, cozy sitting spots for private contemplation. Light tubes were in the roof, to bring in light and vent air and fumes—a simple mechanism to keep out foul weather. This was a beautiful and hallowed place, and women came here for generations.

The closest your time has come to understanding this is in the book The Red Tent, *though ours was not a tent but an actual women's temple: blessed, holy space. We gathered at sacred times of wisdom, the seasonal quarters of the year and cycles of the moon for prayer and devotion. Whether one was dedicated to the path of Spirit, as I was to be, or devoted to home and family, as were most, women came during the time of their monthly moon-blood flow to center on ourselves.*

Moon Time

We knew that during this time, women needed to rest and recuperate to rebalance from the usual caring concerns for others. It is a monthly period (literally) of gathering to naturally withdraw and re-align with our inner being, and with the creator Goddess who is like us.

You may feel this innately, as many do. You live in a culture that has lost this wisdom, and as a result drives women as hard as men. You have products designed to minimize this holy time. You are encouraged to stamp it from awareness or existence, if at all possible.

During the moon flow days, as the women would re-center themselves, the village community would naturally refocus as well. In smaller groups, women would generally bleed in cycle with the moon together, though not all did. Just being in the company of our sisters, those bleeding out of cycle would come into rhythm. There are biological, practical, and spiritual reasons for this, which are interconnected for us. There were women in the village who participated in life as usual. But most of us were together.

This meant that throughout this time, the men and children had a break, too! Rules and practices for prayer, child-rearing, and housekeeping were relaxed. Life was looser and moved in a different time-frame. (Though, in general, time then was much different than we observe now.)

Those who were past bleeding —our wise women—would often join us in the Temple, as this was a time for all to convene. Women are community. We do things as a tribe or in a group. Look at the teenage girls; they are always in a huddle together. Do you not notice that, even now, among your women friends? When you can, you do things together. Tasks and activities were meant to be shared. "Many hands make light work," as the saying goes.

This is practical wisdom, born of biology. We see this sorely lacking in your culture. You become more and more isolated in your separate homes and lives. The issues and diseases of your time are largely all functions of disconnection— with Self, Soul, Source, and sisters.

Rituals of Life

Our "moon time," if you will, is time for us to deeply connect and care for ourselves and each other. It is then that we remember, beyond the busyness (and business) of our daily lives, what really matters and what needs attention. From here we are able to tend and minister to our heart and Soul needs—for ourselves and each other. This is profound nourishment. We see little evidence of this practice of innate care for self and sister in your land. This spiritual act is practical and biological as our bodies, minds, hearts and spirits are united.

There were many rituals and practices of the Temple that were part of our monthly and seasonal cycles. We would come together for these. We also had many traditions that were part of our daily life, which we will share with you. Some are already incorporated in your life and teaching, so you will find them oddly familiar. There are reasons you have been drawn to this path, your calling. The skills you have acquired are no accident, as they are a part of your history throughout your lifeline.

One of these daily practices is the tracking of your hormonal or blood cycle. This one is a key. It is amazing to notice how few women of your day and culture have any awareness of their own bodily rhythms. Tracking your cycle is tremendously empowering, to learn to be aware of your biology and how it relates to mood. This is a potent tool for managing conception and pregnancy—wisdom that has been almost entirely lost. How ironic that this knowledge now seems like quaint folklore, yet in truth it is a key to women's empowerment.

As I digested this experience, I recalled our previous dialogues. I realized that we continued almost exactly where we were previously. With a few reminders, a little bit of overlap, and some embellishment. The repetition was validating and somehow made it feel more real. I felt light, clear, serene, and yet energized by what transpired. I was amazed that it was happening. Our communication also felt totally natural and normal. It felt really right, even destined. Thus we began, yet again.

The Magdalene Path

After that powerful download, I felt profoundly moved. The message from Mary Magdalene impacted me for several days. I kept revisiting her flowing words and crystal-clear images. The visual images were lucid and potent. It was as though I was watching a movie in my mind, with Magdalene narrating. I sensed that I was being invited into something that felt so old, and yet so familiar. I was excited to get back to our dialogue to find out what came next. I no longer felt resistance. I wasn't edgy and distracted, as before. A few days later, with my laptop nearby, I centered myself with deep slow breaths and entered into meditation. Mary Magdalene appeared again and provided some review.

Mary Magdalene: Greetings, dear one. You have walked the "Path of the Mary" for a long time. While there were many Marys in our day, you are most familiar with the ones in your Bible. We were all of a priestess line. That information was omitted by those in the new order who were recording our teachings of The Way of the Magdalene and the Christ. The leaders felt that we needed to be hidden, deemphasized or sublimated, initially for safety reasons. Our mysteries were ultimately forgotten. It is unfortunate that the awareness of who we really were was lost. Though we understand that we were part of a changing time, we never expected to be wiped completely from historical record or memory.

Claire: This is amazing. I feel so blessed for you to come again.

Mary Magdalene: We are delighted that you are here. We speak in the plural, for although it is my voice that you hear, the cumulative culture of the Mari sisterhood is here as well. We are a collective of expanded energy, so there is little sense of separation. We often speak as one. The Magdalene Path is unique and at the apex of our heritage, with a more complete story that will arise.

We are honored at your willingness to endeavor in this task with us. We are hoping that this is something you can keep up with and be done with in a fortnight. But we understand that time has a different meaning and flow in your embodiment. Come to us often. We will keep the line open. Let yourself be surprised at how easy this is. We are delighted on our end, and are working all levels of this project to enhance the flow of output to you and then beyond.

There are many who are interested and waiting for this material. You will be surprised again and again. We will not create a structure or appointments with you, but encourage and advise you to come here as often as you wish and are able. Do not forget that we are waiting. While we will not be annoyed, we will not wait forever. The time is now, for this information is relevant and pertinent. We are not threatening, but know there are other vessels that await, should this prove unproductive.

Claire: No, I want this. I want to do it. I am ready. I know I've dropped this, or "forgotten" this project before. I can't explain why. But I think (and hope) that I am ready now. Please guide me so I hear you clearly and tell your tale as you wish it to be told.

Mary Magdalene: You are of a long line of Mari priestesses, and the Magdalene Path is your home. You have come to share this. Welcome.

I was awestruck when I reviewed this download. I was bursting with gratitude for the opportunity to catch this wisdom as it poured forth, yet again. I had dropped the project before — though with my various life transitions, I could certainly see why. Perhaps I just wasn't ready or it wasn't the right time yet. I was determined not to let it happen again. I felt it strongly in my bones, like a key that unlocked a hidden pledge in my heart.

Essence of Being

Thus my practice of regular connection with Mary Magdalene began. Several times a week, I joined with her in meditation and prayer. Often I had a question about my life or a longing in my heart. Other times, I started *Listening* by asking for guidance that Magdalene wished to share that particular day. Then I typed what I sensed or heard. Mary Magdalene was unwaveringly kind, loving, steadfast, and resolute—a great guide, teacher, and ally. And she was not without her surprises.

Mary Magdalene: It is good to be back with you in this manner. So where do we begin? At the beginning, of course, but that is not where you expect, with my story as The Magdalene. That will come. First, you would perhaps consider this context.

This story begins thousands and thousands of years before we were in the forms we came to known as: women in the cradle of the Middle East. We were largely beings of light and energy, without taking much form. We existed on the planet you know as Earth, though a far different Earth existed at this time. Forms and formlessness were interchangeable. One could come into form and reincarnate in another form, merely with thought and intention. And you are going back to that again…but we digress.

In that era, our formlessness roamed and ruled the planet, moving across the plains and wooded lands as well as mountains, rivers, and oceans. One was in it and yet not entirely of it. The earth herself was forming, with rivers shifting and changing, mountains moving like clay. The Earth herself was forming and reforming, as patterns shifted and settled. It was all coming into being and was not yet solid, as you know it now.

All energies were distinct and discrete, yet easily mutable and changeable. Not like the gaseous energy balls you might envision, but as particles and waves of light and form. We existed as holograms, beings of light and form, both human and angel at once. We were larger, more expansive, and less dense, with bodies of light coming into being in multiple dimensions.

Game of Oneness

Our existence was a process of coming in and out of form for a specific purpose of Soul study, then re-emerging into collective Oneness for the majority of experience. Though very pleasurable and simple, it in fact became so easy that it began to lack appeal. Consciousness, you might say, was becoming bored. There was a consistent urge on the part of the collective—angels you might call them now—to experience more intense and embodied manifestation.

It was observed that there was a lack of ability to fully embrace the experience one was having. That was the purpose of life, after all: to enjoy the full expression of one's particular embodiment. This was the desire, anyway—to come out of spiritual formlessness into form, to taste, feel, sense, touch, hear, and see—and to do it with joy and the awareness that this is all there is. Coming from the formless, it was quite easily accomplished.

Those who incarnated, even in the more intangible form that was the norm of that eon, retained a strong contact with the essence of the Divine, for it was what they knew themselves to be. The identification of a separate self as "I" had not fully formed yet. Incarnation would occur for discrete moments of life experience. Then the embodied one would re-emerge back into the state of Oneness, which was so natural and easily achieved.

The analogy is you swimming in the ocean and being fully part of it, merging your consciousness with "ocean," so it is indistinct from the personal identity of who you are. Then you come out of the ocean to shore for brief moments of time as a unique individual entity, walk around a bit, play on the sand, talk to others, get an ice cream, and then dive back in, returning to Oneness with ocean. You would still have some awareness of a discrete separate personality, but also remember the larger identity as ocean also. You would be part of the whole and one with all, yet unique and separable at will.

This is how the game was played for millennia. It was deeply satisfying and enjoyable—so much so, that at a certain point there started to become a collective urge to retain separation for longer moments. This allowed a fuller exploration of being a unique entity for a longer experience. (Though still not defined as "time" as you know it.) We call this being "in game," when you are currently embodied into form and personality—what you would call a life. It was never intended that the separation from the ocean of Oneness, as we might call it, would be complete and forgotten.

With the dual awareness of separate being and Oneness, it was obvious to those "in game" that the purpose of the experience was to find and learn joy and love. This was the goal always. When one was in form and a so-called challenge or difficulty arose, the game was to recall and remember the Divine in everything and to stay aligned with the Truth in form.

Since the awareness of Oneness was so near, this was relatively effortless to achieve. There was no other option. Challenges of today would not, from that point of view, be perceived as such. There was no forgetting that everything exists in God and Oneness. Today you can easily struggle or suffer from a massive error in memory, forgetting your True Nature.

This seems to be the state that many of you find yourselves in today. You do not recall the Oneness. You forget that the separation into discrete, separate life forms or life times are for the simple expression and experience as a game. In fact, many of you think the game is about creating more and more separation, as is observed in increasing materialism throughout the globe. You long for bigger houses, fancier cars, etc., which create more barriers and less interconnectedness. We note this occurring, even in places that retained a culture of relatedness to Spirit, but suffered more on the physical plane reality, such as India, Asia, and Africa. Acquiring more and more objects generally creates more separation from Truth, as the goal in life becomes about getting, maintaining, protecting, and fearing loss of this "stuff." Even the word "belongings" tells a veiled misperception, as if your objects create belonging.

Between then and now, there was a time when separation and Oneness were remembered differently. Our work here is to remind and reconnect you (and through you, others) to that larger memory of what is true. You do not need to remember it intellectually, or understand it as a concept (though that can be a good place to begin). We hope to invoke a sense of re-merging with the ocean of Oneness. As you come back to your embodied, essence self, you will recall that this is a game for experiencing joy, peace, and will.

Return to True State

There needs to be no experience of hardship—though, when this occurs, there are ways to comprehend the situation that are far different than currently understood. Rather than battling the hardship and efforting to create change, choose the moment of surrender. Recollect Oneness and True State. This is your real life experience, not the one you might be distracted by in the moment.

Recall True State and reconnect with Essence of Being. Once you return to Essence of Being, you remember this is all play for your own learning, growth, and joy. Games are meant to be fun. We do not see your people having nearly enough fun. Go in joy and enjoy! Always! The purpose of life is love and the meaning of life is joy. Follow the path of Joy. No matter what role you are in or the gift you bring, if it is not grounded in love and joy, it is not your True State or purpose.

So whenever you find yourself slogging through an experience or event, ask yourself (and your angels/guides), "What is my True State? Where is the love here? Where is the joy?" It is there, and the sooner you find it, the more fun you will have. As others have said, Earth is the pleasure planet. Though many are seeking pleasure, it is at a superficial, material level, and few are really connecting, finding, and living it as a day-to-day, full-body experience. Find peace, harmony, joy, and love. These are your compass points. Let your inner heart-arrow point and shoot there.

You are loved and you are *love. There is nothing else. All the rest is illusion, created by fear and illusion-filled others who are lost and disconnected. Unfortunately, they are legion in number now. Their version of reality has slowly become predominant, appearing to be the most solid, confident version that exists. This is not so! This is an aberration of the game. We are here to guide you and others out of that morass.*

It is as if you went on a safari, a long journey, and on the way you found an interesting cave tunnel. So seeking shelter, interactions, and interesting adventures on the path of love, you collectively chose to enter this tunnel. Deeper and deeper you went, at first in joy and light, then continuing, for you did not know anything but love.

At some point the light (flames) of your torches became extinguished and you lost sense of the way out. Without the flames of Truth, you thought you needed to figure out with your head which way to go, all on your own. You forged ahead, strong willed and determined, lost in the misperception of your true identity. You forgot that there was another way to go and pushed onward. Deeper and deeper into disconnection, fear, separation, and darkness you went—until now.

Humanity is awakening. After going so deep, the collective game decided "enough" and started to remember another option—or hoped there could be another option. Guides, guardians, and angels on the sidelines of non-physical reality (where you all come from) seeded you with reminders so that at specific times, memory could be evoked. From here, the game starts to turn around. You are collectively on a path back to the light, from the tunnel of isolation and separateness to the ocean of Oneness.

So that is who we are and why we are here. We are not so attached to the story of the Magdalene and Madonna, though we are good guides for remembering. That is what is meant by The Way – the way back home, the way to Oneness and the way to the light. We can share more about how this was done in that timeframe at another sitting. For now we are complete.

Claire: Wow. (I look at my clock and see it's only been an hour.) All this information and yet so little time has passed.

Mary Magdalene: Yes, that is all we need: your open attention, one hour a day. Most days we will be able to conform to that timeframe. When we need more, we can request in advance so that you have the ability to plan. Review later, so if you have questions we can fill in and adjust.

I'm not sure words really captured the awe I felt about what was coming through me. All this came from one hour? Yes. I felt fairly thoughtless and weightless after this session—an unusual experience, to say the least. I spent some time grounding this directive, wondering what I was supposed to do next. I figured it would become clear, fairly soon. But regardless, wow.

Balance of Power Shifts

As I took a shower one morning a few days later, I daydreamed about what the transition time was like. I mused on that formless state Magdalene spoke about, shifting into a time when form was more solid, and then even further to an era when male dominance was taking over. I got a full sense-impression that initially women were involved and in alignment with these shifting roles, as a way to balance power.

Mary Magdalene: There was a time when women and men were in balance with each other and in harmony with nature. This time is so long in the past that it precedes written record or recorded history. Seek other sources to read about those histories, which have been discovered and so aptly represented.

As we have mentioned, during this time it was not uncommon for women to have their temples and ceremonies, practices and rituals to keep their part of the culture alive. Men had their culture also and this practice of keeping separate was not to exclude, but to honor the differences. There were plenty of events, ceremonies, and rituals, as well as daily life, which were cultivated together. There were no feelings of exclusion — of being lesser than or left out. There was full knowledge of each gender's activities, and while they were not always understood, they were accepted.

It was only after invasions and occupations, when the people of the land felt downtrodden and negatively impacted, that this started to create a shift in the region. There was an internal backlash within the culture. During the trauma of this occupation, greater hierarchy of men over women developed as a way for men to exert control and strength over the one area in their lives that they could dominate. The feeling of partnership or equality, which had reigned in the region for millennia, was lost.

The women understood that the dominance of the outsiders was beginning to impact the male psyche, in their ability to lead and provide. Men needed a way to rebalance from the external controls and abuse they were feeling. The women were sensitive to the needs of the men being discounted. Initially, they understood that this new dynamic of masculine empowerment was a means for men to exert power and influence. It was how they could maintain manhood and "save face." But it was never intended to be radically or permanently infused throughout the culture in the way that it was. Nor was such a widespread epidemic of male dominance and control intended. This dynamic we intend to re-balance, repair, and re-pair. But that is for another day.

Priestess Mystery School

As the weeks progressed I got better at orienting myself around this meditation and writing practice that I call *Listening*, but it wasn't perfection. A few mornings passed. I finally centered myself, ready to receive the wisdom of this great being of light, Mary Magdalene. I had no questions or concerns before me. It was a bit like being in a great suspense novel. What will come next? But I wasn't adrenaline-charged or filled with fear. Instead, it felt gloriously easy.

Mary Magdalene: Greetings, we come as a team to welcome you (once again) to our Mystery School. We are Priestesses on the Path of Light. We call this path "The Way," and it has had many names at various times and places: the Isis Mysteries, the Goddess Way, etc. Your point of intersection is through those we call "the Marys."

You know about me, the Magdalene and Mother Mary the Madonna, as well as other Marys who are not as well known: Mary Cleopas, Mary Salome, and Mary Jacobi, for example. You are also aware of others who appear in your Bible, but may not have specific identifiers or names. Mary's mother, Anna, for example, was a Mary as well.

While we were individualized essences, we were interchanged in the telling of tales because we worked as a group. (Also our culture was shifting to the marginalizing of women's experience.) It was not our individual identities that were of importance anyway. What was important were the teachings of The Way. How we experienced ourselves as people was quite different in our time than yours. Our individualized consciousness was not so solid, so our attachment to our identity as human beings was not so strong, like it is now. Consciousness was expressed differently. We shall explain that in a bit.

Anointer, Teacher, Leader

So, in fact, while we did exist, it is not of great importance to us who did what where: the washing of feet or anointing of oils. We were attempting to tell a tale and point to what is hidden or veiled. We knew our value and worth, and whose roles were whose. As Magdalene, I was a great teacher and leader. I was the anointer, the bride to the chosen bridegroom. All were aware of this mystery teaching. It never occurred to us that this identity would be so badly damaged and the knowledge that I carried would be twisted, subverted, and ultimately lost.

Naturally, we had no idea how our story would be retold thousands of years hence. We were not thinking that far ahead! I knew there was a mystery teaching being played out that would be obvious to some and hidden from others. Such is the way with stories—some get it and some do not. It is up to the receiver which story they hear and understand.

The same situation can be observed (or experienced) by five different persons, and each will have an entirely different perception of the event. Each will have various interpretations of the cause, reason, and meaning of the event, which lead to differing reactions: feeling elated as victor or dejected as victim. It is all a matter of perspective. This is well known, and yet the potent impact of this truth is just being unwrapped, like a valuable gift that has lain untouched on the table for hundreds and thousands of years.

Unveiling the Bride

Part of the reason for our coming to you is to tell a different tale from the same story. We wish to unveil what has been hidden. It is time for the unveiling of the Bride to the Beloved. We are so used to the common story that it is difficult, nary impossible, to view it in a new way. And this is why we seek you to tell this tale.

While it is important to know we existed as teachers, it is not as critical to know who did what, where, and when, at this point. That will become obvious when necessary and remain veiled when it is not. You are familiar with the commonplace version as well as research on a variety of views. We will not rehash old stories that are common in your Bible. That is for others. Hence, it is correct that it is no longer helpful to read the writings of others on this topic, to avoid clouding your view so that you perceive our story clean and fresh.

I felt uneasy about this Divine Download. I was confused about the relative importance or unimportance of Mary Magdalene and the other women she mentioned. Magdalene responded to my unspoken concern about how a new perspective would be received.

Mary Magdalene: We urge you not to worry about the message and how it will be received, at this point. We wish you let us be the guide and you be the boat, so to speak. The material will emerge in a fully fashioned manner without your needing to control. Let us have a turn telling that which needs to be told, and let the sorting and sifting take care of itself later, as it will.

Prophesy Fulfilled

A few days passed. After reviewing this passage some questions lingered. How could Magdalene and the others NOT be important? Was her identity really irrelevant or interchangeable with her companions? What was I missing? I laid this in Magdalene's lap when I sat and meditated next.

Claire: I am confused. I thought I understood quite clearly that, Magdalene, you anointed Jesus (Yeshua) with the oil on his head and feet. Though your identity is somewhat veiled, the event is well reviewed in the Bible, one of the few stories mentioned in all four of the traditional Gospels. I understand this was a symbolic ritual act, in keeping with your tradition, signaling the prophesy that Jesus was intended to fulfill as messiah.

You served in your role as the bride to the beloved. As Goddess/High Priestess/Queen, you anointed your God/consort/bridegroom/King. You were charged with making this symbolic act which had a long historical and mythical tradition in your land. This foretold his death and resurrection, in keeping with an ancient religious prophesy. If I understand correctly now, you are saying who did this is not important and that you were all interchangeable? It seems the focus of this project has been about reimagining and revealing the truth of your existence to the world. Am I missing something or receiving this inaccurately? This does not seem to fit with the importance of restoring your name or "reclaiming the bride and beloved to restore the wasteland," mentioned earlier, which I thought was the foundation of this work.

Mary Magdalene: Relax, dear one. Indeed, we are sorry you are confused. I do want to assure you it is I, Miri-Am the Magdalene, here with you. I am always with you, and you are with me as well. We are one, but not in the way you imagine. It is confusing to translate from my inter-dimensional reality into yours, but I will try, as it relates to the question at hand.

Our beings intersect in light through holographic dimensions of reality that you are currently unable to perceive. Trust that we are connected through time in lives where we have been in form together. You and I are priestesses of old. And you have served me, and I, you. We are equals in stature, though we take different stations in different embodiments or lifetimes.

As such, I am no longer in a place where it is important to state for my ego/ persona, "look at me, I did this thing." My point of perception is no longer attached to identity. While in fact it may be true, it is no longer personally relevant for me to take credit. What is important is that the anointing occurred, the template was set and the prophesy was satisfied. Was I his bride? Symbolically, yes, though in a formal sense, no. Were we partners? Yes, absolutely. He was the King, I was the Queen.

I do wish to convey that the anointing was heralded. It was acknowledged by all. In that act, I became his bride; this was symbolic, for the people needed to see this for the prophesy to be fulfilled. And so it was. For me, it is not so much about being acknowledged as the bride, 2000 years later, and you taking this up a cause, as if to right some wrong. That is a stand to be taken by others.

Rather, my teachings are what I wish to feed you: for women and men to have an embodied experience of the sacred, in this lifetime. That is what is important—not to review and rehash the old news. Move on to the new, the untold tales, sister of the light. You will find more sustenance there, perhaps surprisingly so.

Hidden Mysteries

The Awakening Divine Feminine project was starting to feel really juicy and exciting. I had no idea where Magdalene's story was going. I knew there were big gaps in my awareness. That was okay. I trusted that it was unfolding as it needed to.

Several days after the last download, I sat with my small pot of tea, surrendered my breath and attention, which stilled and centered into *Listening*. I opened my heart and crown, and prayed my request for Magdalene to come. She shared the following:

Mary Magdalene: Today I wish to clarify the role or position I held as the Magdalene. This was not a name, but rather a title held by a woman in a position of spiritual leadership in the Temple and community. While I am well known as "the" Magdalene, there have in fact been many. As High Priestess of the Temple, I was not the only Magdalene, though I am the most well-known. In fact, I was leader of many called Miri-Am or Mari-Anna, a title meaning "holy" or "good." We have discussed the Mari (or Mary) priestesses previously.

In the time of Yeshua becoming the Christ, there was a class of women who were part of the Hebrew faith. We followed a path of the inner circle, intermingling practices from the mysteries of Isis. There is strong lineage of Goddess cultures in these lands, which intermixed liberally at that time. With cultures moving about nomadically through the Middle East, it was not uncommon. There were no lines drawn in the sand.

So while the names may differ — Astarte, Ashera, Inanna, Ishtar, Isis, Alat, (even Aphrodite and Diana) — the essence is the same. Naturally this is left-over from eons in Egypt and other tribal Middle Eastern nation-states. These practices were woven into the culture of women. It was veiled from men and remains hidden to those who are looking in the traditional official documents of Judaism.

These are the inner mysteries of women that have been created and handed down from elder to daughter, a secret inner life of women that is created in such a heavily patriarchal, hierarchical state—which is why you have never heard more. If you start to look, notice, and ask, you will start to see and understand.

These are the mysteries of the Red Tent. There are secret tales of those times, but under the lens of the dominant cultural eye, they are rarely revealed—never to common outsiders.

The Goddess culture flourished for thousands of years in that region. It is only natural that the ancient customs would be subsumed into the newer or revised spiritual traditions as they emerged. It is also just as understandable that the parts that could not be integrated and assimilated would continue but be kept hidden. And that is where our story unfolds.

The Way

Tonight we wish to speak to you of my role as the Magdalene on the path called "The Way." As previously mentioned, Magdalene is a title which has become my name. I am one of many. There have been many that have held this lineage, whether they knew it or not. And of those who knew they carried the title, few bore it in the world, though they may have worn it in their hearts.

There are many on planet Earth today who follow the calling and hold the Magdalene Path in their heart center. This way of being is cultivated from the Magdalene, and it is full of God: goodness, gratitude, and grace, the 3 G's. While heart-centered, it is not cloying, sweet, or sentimental. Those on this path are strong, while full of compassion, wisdom, and the desire to do good for the sake of doing what is right for all.

So while loving, the energy of the Magdalene is not always gentle or soft. While it is kind, it is not always easy. Those who bear this do not have an easy path, for it is a path of wisdom, truth, and strength, and this is often worn like a sword. The tongue can be sharp: beware the barbs.

Partnership with Yeshua

I sensed that there was some context and backstory about Magdalene's relationship with Jesus that I probably needed to dive into. I avoided this immensely. I've never felt a strong connection to Jesus, whether that was despite of or because of being raised Catholic. I have long sensed that the true story got twisted (along with Magdalene's), to serve religious power and political rule. It seemed likely, after all the changes and translations of The Bible, that Jesus' real teachings got lost or distorted. As a result, many have died in his name. That seems a perversion of what he called The Way, his message of Love and Light. And I was irritated about that.

Given my obviously unorthodox beliefs and perspective about Mary Magdalene as a great teacher, leader, and healer (rather than the typical version of her as a sinner and prostitute), I'm not even sure I would call myself Christian —not as people today know it. I believe Jesus was a remarkable teacher, healer, and leader: a great way-shower. But I also think his teachings have largely been misconstrued. Yet the dynamic between Jesus and Magdalene is a critical part of Magdalene's story. I felt the pull of this relationship pretty strongly. I should not have been surprised when it came up quickly in our Divine dialogue.

Claire: I have felt you calling to me all day. Finally, I am here. So what parts need to be shared? What needs to be written of this "greatest story never told"?

Mary Magdalene: Yes, beloved, we are happy to meet with you. There is nothing yet told of the pairing of masculine and feminine through Yeshua and myself, and how it impacted the healings. Our partnership was the key to the kingdom, and this has been lost. Even when others tell my tale, they lose sight of the relationship and the convergence of energy and light that occurred when we came together. This was meant to be a new model for how women and men relate. This was radical then and is still not the normative. We sense you are tired, perhaps now is not the time.

Claire: I am tired, and yet if not now, when? It might never happen.

Mary Magdalene: It is and it will. We will stay with you until you surrender. We don't mean that as a threat, dear. We are not pressuring. Surrender is not a submission or position of weakness, but a place of strength and power. It is an open-armed stepping up and allowing in. Of Listening and partnering with Spirit. It is part of the Path.

Claire: Okay, so about your partnership with Yeshua…

Mary Magdalene: Yes. The traveling and healing that we all did in Judea and afterward through the Cathars in France. There is a connection here to the original pairing of Adam and Eve. His first partner got lost, too, you know. Lilith has been virtually written out of that story, except as a "side note" — the bad girl. See the connection?

Claire: Interesting, yes. We are taught the basic story of Adam and Eve as the basis of Genesis, the beginning of creation. But there was a beginning before that. Adam's original mate was Lilith, who was a Goddess and was discarded for a more sanitized (though definitely still "bad") wife, Eve. I don't know anything about Lilith except she was a "bad girl." If Adam and Eve were the first people, as commonly told, how could Lilith come *before* Eve? Puzzling. It makes no sense. (This is where my lack of knowledge about the Bible hinders me.) Jesus similarly lost his partner—also labeled "bad girl" as a fallen woman—and in a way became spiritually "coupled" with Virgin Mary, as icons. This has always seemed odd and icky; that mother-son pairing seemed too ethereal, enmeshed, and (dare I say) incestuous. In some versions of Christianity, he's married to "the mother church" (an interesting turn of phrase).

I really get a sense that we've missed the true meaning and magic of Jesus's power by losing that relational partner connection. He was a teacher, a rabbi, who was a bachelor, which was unheard of in ancient Israel. We lost the energy dynamic (and role modeling) between him and his sacred consort, his bride and beloved, Magdalene. Half of the whole is missing.

Mary Magdalene: Indeed. Later we will discuss the Divine Masculine, and how it relates to Sacred Union and Hieros Gamos, the ancient holy rite of partnering. No wonder your divorce rates are epidemic, you've misplaced this sacred aspect of the contract. For now, I want to focus on the healing power of the Divine pairing, for it impacts your culture and relationships today. Let me introduce you to my mate.

Claire: Jesus? Really?

I noticed an energy shift that was subtle, but palpable. Difficult to describe except to say the signature was different. It was more masculine—linear, strong and clear—though still soft, expansive, and loving.

Jesus: Yeshua, yes. In the beginning, I was very scared. After all, I had heard about the Temple and her priestesses. The young ones in training were in service to the Great Goddess who gives us all life. I, as a male, was in service to the One God. This was how it was in our time, though this is now largely forgotten.

Many women of the Temple were known far and wide for their different skills in weaving, dye-craft, and psychic and healing arts, but none had the renown of the Magdalene. As a leader, she was a strong yet gentle being, known for wisdom beyond her years.

Long ago, I had been chosen to study with her, and this was unusual, being an adult male, just barely past puberty. But mine was not your usual destiny. I had spent the last seven years of my life in many foreign lands, living with different peoples, tribes, and countries, learning the secret teachings and Wisdom of the Ages.

I spent many hours exploring with different masters as my guides. I was young and open. I could hold and move energy, weaving and healing with the light. I learned to channel this energy stream from God, known as Allaha (in our Aramaic), but who I called Abba (which you would translate as Papa or Daddy). This was the most fun and so enjoyable.

I learned about the light and how it heals, even when I bring it through my ineffective and miniscule vessel. There is a channel with a way to access it that is nonspecific. It requires no sacrifices or obedience to church dogma. It is available to people of all paths, faiths, nations, and races. This path of healing with light knows no boundaries, as it is a path of love, of home. I came here to show you all that this magic is yours, too.

People enjoyed watching the healings. The sick felt better, they were happy to see me. I showed them how they, too, could do this. Often the people did not want to learn; they wanted me to do it for them. I told them it was theirs to do, too. They claimed I had special powers, yet I knew I came here to share them. It was most curious that they would raise me up as a God. I protested, "No, no, you too can do this," and they would scoff and claim me "Master." The humility I was known for was merely my inability to accept gifts and talents I could not take credit for. I knew this was from the Father, the masters and the high ones up above. This was not of me, just through me. It was theirs to claim, too.

I will again try to show you. Open to the healing light, sense it. You just have to trust your own way. It will not be his way or hers. Those ways may look easy, but they are not to the one living it. Each has her own travels and travails. Each is on her own path. Yours is yours alone. Don't measure against another, for someone always has to come up smaller or better than the other. No one is a winner when one is a loser. Rejoice in the variety and quantity of guidance that is all around. Know that it is "all good" and all for you. All of it is part of your path. Remember, trust your knowing and Listening.

Claire: What about the healing practices that Magdalene alluded to, will you share those?

Yeshua: *Indeed. At first it was awkward between us. We had played together when we were milklings. We were similar in age, though our training had been vastly different and our status and renown were both great. Our coming together was prophesied since we were young children, so there was great tension about it.*

Claire: Milklings? That's not a term I recognize.

Yeshua: *When we first met, we were children of nursing age — toddlers, you might call us. But many moons and many ceremonies had passed until we met again. And so there was distance and our roles. We were no longer children playing together. But I will not forget the moment we met. I was brought to her audience in the Temple, to begin our lessons together. She was to teach me. Later, I would share with her what I learned from the world beyond the Temple walls, which she knew little of at that point.*

I was brought to the Hall of the Mari, the Temple's throne room, filled with brilliant light the color of the most vivid gems. She sat waiting regally, like the Queen she was. She greeted me warmly. She was a woman of incredible bearing and grace, her presence and beauty held me captive. Her energy field was clear, bright, and enormous—unlike anything I had ever experienced before (or since). She was quite personable. Our first meeting was easy and convivial, much to the surprise of the waiting eyes and ears of the Temple community. I was awestruck. And I immediately bonded to her heart. Regardless of the path our destinies would force us to take, we were One in this moment of meeting and our connection never waned.

From there, it was quite simple for us to engage and share the healing practices of sound, light, and energy. She drew from her Temple training, and I from my own lineage and travels abroad. We had an instant bond of love, regardless of our prearranged pairing. Our connection, along with the adept wisdom of the ages, was (and is) a remarkable force for healing and goodness.

Together we could do anything. From that moment forward, regardless of the paths our lives took us in the physical plane, energetically we have never been separate. That is the irony, that in my dying and resurrection, we are still bonded. Regardless of the way the story has been manufactured and manipulated, we are still one. The priests in authority can deny this, but she is with me always.

Claire: Wow, that's powerful. Thank you, Yeshua.

Yeshua: So the healing I did, we did. We practiced tandem healing. It was always in relation to each other, using love and light. The tools and processes she and I shared, we would simply do in sync, as follows. We would center ourselves first and then synchronize our breath. Then we created an energetic connection, like a bridge of flowing love and sparkling light between us. Next, we opened the channel to Spirit. This created a field of potential or possibility. Finally, we flowed that energy between us to the one (or ones) in need. You might notice it as the shape of a cross.

We would blanket our intended "patient" with a shower of stars, raining light and love through and around them. This would charge the field that surrounds them with infinite potential and possibility so that it felt alive, electric. Even at a distance, this could be done. This was the case in 100% of the so-called miracles that others tell about me. Magdalene's presence was simply removed from the record because of the practices and beliefs of the culture at that time. That is it: a fairly simple process, but vastly under-utilized or explored.

Claire: Wow, again I am blown away. It sounds so simple and elegant, obviously so potent. Thank you.

Yeshua: *Thanks to you, I bow to you in gratitude for taking up this project.*

Claire: You are so welcome. The pleasure is mine, finally!

I noticed afterward that my feelings about Jesus softened (to say the least) from our interaction. How could they not? My distaste and anger about Jesus (and Christianity, in general) faded. I realized that it's not his fault what others have done with his teachings. We can't control the story others have about us. I viscerally felt the compassion and non-attachment he felt about this. While we did not speak about this, I imagined he was as dismayed and disappointed as I—probably even more so.

Refuge in Egypt

One week later, I returned to commune with Magdalene. After my connection with Jesus, I was curious about where our dialogue would go next. A part of me was apprehensive about what I experienced with him, since that gets into touchy religious territory. I lacked any clear, compelling questions, though, so I centered myself and opened to her guidance. The next Divine Download began.

Mary Magdalene: Yes, I am here. There is more content available. The next piece to convey is about our time in Egypt, in Alexandria. This was an interesting time in our lives—the Mari sisters, myself, and the children. Indeed there were many children, not only mine. And many of the women had mates who were partners in life and love, too.

After our ordeal with the Christ, his descent into death and back into glory of life (a tale that is well addressed in various mythos), we left our home. It was a dark and challenging time, of course. We traveled with my Uncle, Joseph of

Arimathea. He was a wealthy merchant and a Guide of high regard within the inner mysteries of Kabbalah. As part of our inner circle, he was duty-bound to protect me and the child I carried within. Due to his positions of wealth, power, and prestige, he was able to smuggle us away. Our little entourage included the children and our sisters, the other Mari, and a few men.

While there is much that can be said of that time, I am most interested in sharing with you about the practices we learned and used from the great Temples there.

By this time, the religions of Egypt and Judea were distinct, of course, but after so many years of crossover, there were beliefs and practices that were incorporated. The Egyptians had a great culture of healing, using sound, light, and gems to augment, enhance, or shift energy. Of course, our physical bodies were not as dense as yours now, so therefore those modalities had greater impact than one might expect in your modern world. In addition, the Egyptians were renowned for their understanding of the energetics of physical space, architecture, and the healing powers of plants. These were quite different than commonly understood or practiced today.

This was a great boon to us, as we were able to use these techniques to repair and rejuvenate from our ordeal. We incorporated their wisdom into our healing meditations. Much of what you are learning today comes from that stream, using light, sound, and color to heal. This is still vastly under-used in your age, but the knowledge is returning. We wish to share tools and practices, using color, breath, and light, later in our dialogue.

Our little traveling family spent many sun cycles (or "years") in Egypt in the progressive intellectual center of Alexandria. Here, there were many of our faith. We had community and family, so we felt safe to heal. After a time, it became apparent that the western shores and distant lands were calling to us. For what reason, we knew not. But we felt summoned, so off we went.

Boat without Oars

After the sections about Yeshua (Jesus) and then Egypt, I was really hooked. I was fascinated by where the story would go next. It was taking some interesting twists and turns. I prayed and inwardly asked Magdalene to come. I wondered if she had more "herstory" to share. Immediately, I felt her immense presence: a sweet sensation like a warm, gentle breeze settling over and inside me.

Mary Magdalene: There is much lore of our travel to France in "a boat with no oars." This is metaphor, meaning we were not steering, since we had no idea where we were going. We were guided by Spirit and just knew we were headed toward Gaul (your France), and then onward from there to Brittany in the North and on to Britannia. We were so thrilled! To see new lands and new people, this was exciting. And to do so under my wise uncle's protective (and well-resourced) wing was sheer delight. Of course, we were also saddened and scared, as any new journey is bound to bring fear. But we were calm in knowing we were in alignment with the will and wishes of our creator who had been guiding us for so long.

We traveled by sea for many days, and our comforts were few. We took turns holding watch, not merely for seafaring purposes, but to hold the High Watch of our intention and alignment. We knew that this was what mattered most. By setting our intention (as we will share later), we shot an arrow toward our chosen destination, which was not a place as much as a destiny. While we did not know where we were going, we sensed that we were going toward something.

So we intended ourselves in the direction of the light and hope that drew us. Those among us with direct access to guidance from God knew where to head, and the rest trusted. We all shared skills and abilities, but there were healer-teachers of an advanced degree among us in the inner circle. We sought a new community who awaited us. We understood this was where our ministry of The Way was to land next. The Way of Light and Love is our practice, the New Covenant that Yeshua (your Jesus) is known for in your time.

Thus we sailed forth in "the boat with no oars" and landed on the fine shore of southern Gaul, near where what is now Marseille. What a lovely land! There was a warm orange glow. The fruit, the light, the orchards of pear and plum were all so magnificent. The land was unlike any place we had been before, with soft rolling hills and a horizon marked by the spikes of tall trees reminiscent of cypress in Judea. We disembarked here and began to weave ourselves into the life of the people.

We were welcomed as we shared our gifts and blessings. The women were very open to the Mari sisters and me. While some were of our faith (Nazarene-Essene Jews), many were not. They adored our child, now nearing womanhood, Sarai, often called Sarah the Egyptian. Of course she is Egyptian, for she was born and came from there! But her lineage is royal, from Yeshua and myself. She was recognized as a child of prophesy and treated as an angel. She was loved and is love.

We lived in community for many years, and in time my friendship with one person in particular grew. Maximin was a great guardian and guide for us, helping us with our mission in many ways. He was a great man and a love, but none was ever going to replace Yeshua (who you know as Jesus) in my heart and Soul. Some have wondered if he was either Yeshua in disguise or my new mate, but he was neither. Maximin is not to be underestimated, though his true story has never been told. Now is not the time for that. Suffice to say, we could not have done what we did, living in the wilderness, without him.

He was unparalleled in his commitment and affection for The Way. Indeed, he first found the cave (which became known as Sainte Baume) that we were to make our home. This is no small place, and in fact a community was easily created there in the rock and bones of that mountain. While it is known as "my" home, it is where I lived with my daughter and community of sisters who were studying the path of light. A place of spiritual study and refuge, it would now be considered a monastery or convent, which it eventually became. We lived here for many years very happily, and it is a holy place in my heart.

Joseph, my uncle, left shortly after arriving, once he understood we were safe and well cared for. He traveled with my youngest son. They went on to Chartres, in Brittany, for some time before heading to Glastonbury and Avalon in Britannia. After delivering our "grail prince," he returned there for many long years. A man of deep paradox, my uncle and his peers were engaged in their own sacred mysteries, which relate to the holy box.

Claire: What is the Holy Box—the Ark of the Covenant?

Mary Magdalene: Not exactly. The Holy Box is the Holy Sepulcher. It was akin to "the Holy of Holies." It was a container (like a trunk) that held our sacred documents and personal treasures from our life with Yeshua. Sacred books and writings, not yet (but becoming) revealed in your time. Those that were not with my uncle were with me. The Order of the Holy Sepulcher included those few men, including Luke (of the Gospels), who were charged to serve and protect the contents. Being a man of wealth, commerce and high regard, he naturally took to travelling.

On his travels, my uncle would, of course, visit his charges (I, my daughter, and our Mari sisters). He spoke of a mystical isle of women—healers and priestesses devoted to the light. He loved Avalon and spoke longingly of returning whenever he could. His fervor for this magical place was so strong that he was convincing of my need to go. I knew it was my destiny to visit there and deliver my daughter, Sarai.

I felt very pleased and somewhat surprised that our dialogue turned in this direction. I secretly wondered if there would be any information from Magdalene about France. I've long had a deep fascination for this region. Then I heard legends of Mary Magdalene having lived there. Was it just a myth?

A few years before, I'd been blessed to travel with a small group on a spiritual pilgrimage to explore France and see for myself if her legend was still evident there. And I found images of her everywhere. Her veneration was profuse. I was so thrilled to receive this guidance from Magdalene as validation of what I experienced there, to confirm this as Truth. And then Magdalene shared more:

Moving On

Mary Magdalene: So off we went, our group of 13, to find this glorious place. And find it, we did. But first, we travelled to Chartres. It was not known as that then, nor was the magnificent cathedral — a grand monument to love and the mysteries of the Divine Feminine — there yet. This was long held as a sacred place, with a magical grove and a blessed spring (which became a well and then the cathedral crypt). It was a spiritual learning center of great renown even when we visited.

No surprise that it became the haven of the Sacrament that it is. What a marvel to behold the energy of the place, from the powerful land and its sweeping views. The glory of the sacred labyrinth, holy ground. It is long-revered by those who worship the Goddess, in whatever form and by whatever name she is known, regardless of religion or spiritual ideology. Such is the reason for the many representations of Our Lady and the Black Madonna, for we are all one regardless of our outer accoutrements.

Wherever we would go, we would teach. We would arrive someplace and devote our days to living life. It was an easy, simple existence, far different from your lives today. Nights we sat around a hearth or open fire, sharing and healing. Those lessons are contained in this manuscript. Our principal and primary tool is light and aligning to the grace and guidance of God (which you may call Spirit or Source). We knew that God was not a he or a she, but was manifest in both forms. This is largely what got us (and our people, the Cathars, much later) in trouble with the ruling fathers of the church, as this vision of shared divinity was considered heretical. In some places, this would still be so.

Avalon Sisters

Eventually, we pushed on to Avalon. What a glorious sight to behold. Beauty was all around, again unlike anything previous in our days. The soft light cast a pallor of grey from fog and stone over the rolling curves of the emerald land.

It was deep and mystical from the moment we set foot there. We knew we found a special place. It was almost like living in a dream and difficult to convey. The light was softly golden and sparkling, with no direction or source. Everything seemed lighted from below or within. It was curious and took us time to orient.

In Avalon, it seemed as though days and nights were switched. The days were short and nights were long. Much living was done in the dim of night. Light was low; there never seemed to be full sun. There were a few glorious days of summer when we played, frolicked, and rejoiced.

The buildings were chilled, made of stone as they were. But the smooth squares were a comfort to the feet, so worn they were from centuries of travel. The hearths were large and the ceilings were low, with roofs made of thatch straw as well as timber (which was not so plentiful). The insides were filled with simple but elegant housewares, comfortable furnishings with fabrics that seemed ancient and exotic to us. The lighting was remarkable, with lanterns and sconces that were lit from no particular fuel other than the mind's clear intention.

The structures were rounded and had a cozy feel, huddled together with paths and covered walkways for ease in the miserable weather. The plants and grasses that covered their fair isle were remarkable, with flowers in the spring to delight us for an eternity of learning. Apple blossoms forever filled the air with a scent so magnificent I could never forget it. And there were herbs aplenty in this rich, moist environment.

The air seemed to be all moisture and no heat. For those of us used to a Mediterranean climate, this difference was huge. Bundle as we did, some of us could never get warm. Were it not for our special skills of directing energy and creating heat, we would have been severely challenged. As it was, some never adjusted, and in time chose to leave this otherwise charmed place.

Despite these seemingly inhospitable conditions, I loved it there. We could not have found a better home. We were welcomed warmly by the sisterhood who inhabited this mystical land. Our camaraderie with the Avalon priestesses was immediate and deep. The acknowledgement of Soul sisterhood was keen and rewarding. These women were small and delicate, with a beauty that was otherworldly. We certainly understood the "glamour" of the isle after seeing her inhabitants. Many were born there. Others were promised to their Goddess when they were young, as we were to the Temple like in our native land. Some chose to stay, while others would leave, marry, and live a family life. But once from the Isle, you were always from the Isle. These women lived a special "normal" life, with the skills and talents they learned as priestesses woven into their everyday lives. Eventually it became dangerous and even deadly to practice such skills—a sad time, indeed.

We were able to learn their mysteries and teach them ours. As we shared, we often laughed with wonder at the similarity of our teachings and practices. While sometimes the methods would be different (certainly the herb and plant lore was), it was noted that a thread of Oneness wove through all of us as women. I adored the young ones and felt glory in my heart to open them to the light and love of The Way. I knew they would carry it in their hearts to the countless generations that came after them.

I lived there for three cycles of the sun and moon, long enough to teach our priestess sisters the mysteries of our Grail. We taught about the power of Love, which they were not new to. These women were incomparable healers and teachers. I gleaned as much as I gave. Their herb and faerie lore was a new lineage of wisdom, and yet I felt as much at home as in the desert Temple of my youth. It was a time of great richness and wonder, as I had found a new community of sisters so unlike myself and yet so similar. I am told I left my mark there, as well my daughter. My teachings have become interwoven in a way that no one would suspect. This makes me smile.

This was a place where the veil between the worlds was thin. Access to spirit was easy and palpable. So to get there, you had to know how to move energy and matter to part the veils with light. This was a new form for us, but not unachievable.

With us we brought Sarai, my daughter, who early on in our visit identified Avalon as her final home. While it tore my heart asunder to leave her there, I knew it was her calling. Her teachings and prophesy wove into their lives in a way that it could only be seen as the destiny path it was. It was as if she was a Celtic maid from the start and we were delivering her to her place of power. It is a wonder, though perhaps no surprise, that the knowledge of her presence and her message did not survive there. It does, but it is hidden. Her memory lives in the heart of the lineage she bore.

The teachings of Avalon did not survive intact themselves, and that is a shame. These mystical branches did not survive far from the trunk of the tree of orthodoxy as well as we hoped or planned. Many are not aware of my travels to Avalon, and yet it is a wonder. The local traditions and symbols that are known and recognized are similar — not to mention the lineages of red hair so like to mine.

Claire: I wanted to ask about that. What about Sarai, was she dark-haired as I've seen her depicted, or red-headed? You are usually portrayed with red hair, it seems. Is that for real?

Mary Magdalene: Yes, Sarai had the red hair, as did I. She was called "the Egyptian," and so it has been assumed that she was dark like those people. She was called "dark and swarthy," not typically because of her skin (which was olive) or hair color, but because she was hidden or in shadow. She was veiled, especially in travel. As the fruit of my union with Yeshua, she was the precious gem, a secret to be protected at all cost. She is the Grail Princess. This is why so little is known about her now. The practice of keeping her secret was so well maintained that it became a hard habit to break. She is only known among the fringes of society, initiates of the inner circle. Now it is time for the inner and outer circles to shift and be known. It is time for the unveiling of Truth and Light.

Circles of Wisdom

The teachings of Avalon were imbedded in light. The challenge is how to maintain the mysteries of this light over eons of darkness. It is a pedagogy of the Matrix, the Divine Code within. This advanced teaching is not for all, which is just as well, for not all are ready or interested.

There are circles within circles of wisdom. Some teachings are of the outer world, for those who exist solely on the material plane. There is a density and tangibility to these types of teachings. These outer forms would not be called mysteries, for they are not of the unseen realms. They are the most basic level of knowledge, for the majority of seekers. Most are complacent, readily happy to accept the commonplace answers for what is seen by the eye and felt by the hand. This is fine, for this is where these Souls are in their evolutionary journey to Oneness. It is all about that journey. We are all moving through our own classroom towards the next lesson, the next step of Oneness.

Then there are inner teachings. Even they are in layers. Different paths have different access points and levels. Many now are searching for deeper and deeper layers, but do not have the access points. This is where a master or teacher comes in, as you hold keys to portals that the uninitiated cannot unlock. It is not about privilege or prestige, but about safe passage and gaining access to knowledge that would be hazardous if used incorrectly.

Such is the case with Avalon. As time went on, the access points became thin and harder to reach, though not for a lack of trying. With passing time, the knowledge faded and eventually was lost from a lack of belief. The teachers were fewer and challenges were greater. Interest was lost. We entered times of greater density, when Avalon all but disappeared, retained only by a brave few. Now the journey to Avalon must be taken on inner realms. (Though there are still some guides who can take you in the physical.) These mystical paths are accessible, but only to seekers, the initiates, and the High Guard.

It is important to speak of and understand this connection with Avalon, for it is part of the Magdalene lineage. Notice that, often, those drawn to my mysteries are inexplicably pulled there, too. There is an incredibly obvious reason, which you have just learned: I was there. Some have suspected, while others will not be surprised. And still others will refute and doubt. That is no matter. There is a Oneness to the teachings, message, and mysteries that is infused across the geography of time and locale. And the mysteries of Avalon are ours, too. Welcome home.

This message was long, but so deeply nourishing and delicious. And such a surprise! Much of what Magdalene shared I had never known. It all felt so Soul-right and confirming. As I worried (a bit) that others would refute my information, I became clear: I can't do anything about what others think. This download felt aligned and congruent as Truth. So I practiced staying present to the beauty that was being revealed to me.

Beyond the Mists

I was feeling antsy to get the Divine Downloads completed, though I sensed there was much more to come. A week or so later, I sat in my usual spot, with a cup of tea by my cozy couch. I entered meditation and requested that Magdalene share any words of wisdom she wished. I sensed her presence instantly, and my edgy nerves were immediately calmed, softly and lovingly. Before I mentioned it, she once again intuited and addressed the stress I felt:

Mary Magdalene: We understand that you feel pressure to get this material out to the world. But understand this is much like birthing a baby; this process has its own timing. A premature birth can end the life of the child or create big challenges in those early days, to say the least. Trust that you are gestating something big that will take its own time. Rushing that time will not make it come any sooner or any better. In fact, it could have quite the opposite effect. Just trust and roll with the flow.

Today we wish to speak to you again of that time before time, when the mists of Avalon had not yet closed. The part you are missing and that you fail to comprehend is that all time is seamless and connected. So when you think about Avalon being before or after another time period in your so-called history, you miss the true essence of that place. It is timeless.

As you have surmised, there is a connection between those in Avalon and the Maris (or Marys) in the lineage of Mary Magdalene, not just in your heart, but in the lineage of teachings. This knowledge traveled from Palestine (what is now Israel), into Egypt, through Gaul (France), north to Brittany and across to Britain to the land of Myrrdin (or Merlin) in Glastonbury and Avebury.

Many have speculated that Joseph of Arimethea traversed that course. In fact, his walking stick was planted in the Abbey at Glastonbury. Also whispered but largely unknown is that he traveled with and delivered one of the bloodline children, the son of the Christ and myself, the Magdalene. What is hidden, but contemplated by some (such as yourself) is that I was there as well, which we spoke of previously. In fact, I lived many years on and off the Isle of Avalon.

Claire: Why is this not known? Why is this information lost?

Mary Magdalene: Much of what you know and believe from your masculine-based culture is untrue. Information that has been passed forth has been altered and changed. The patriarchal church Fathers were (and are) quite thorough and convincing in their ability to dismember information that was not in keeping with the message and "truth" they wished to press forth.

You know this is true, as there are many Gospels that were removed in the Fourth century. What is unknown is how much was removed previously. With the burnings of the library in Alexandria centuries before that, sacred knowledge was lost or appears to be omitted. We predict these and other documents will be recovered shortly, within your lifetime, as the scrolls from Qumran (which we spelled Qumrn) or Nag Hammadi have been unearthed. Goddess is giving back her Truth to those who are seeking and now ready to find. The Earth and her people are ready.

So this is why it is unknown: It was forcibly suppressed. Thousands were killed in the South of France (and other places) to eliminate this path, and it has happened countless times before and since. It is not so much about censoring the truth of the bloodline (though that is so), but of the message and practices that were part of The Way. It is the remembering of this path that we bring for you to receive and share.

Now, back to our story. So we were in Avalon: you and I, along with Mari Anath, Mari Grieg, and countless others. These are names you do not know because they were so expertly erased. Lacking tangible evidence is a means of discounting the accuracy of this message and the truth it speaks. Beware of this tactic, in yourself or others.

Some of our group were safely left behind (such as Mary Jacobi and Mary Salome) in the south of France. And their story, skills, and gifts are largely lost also. Some women chose to move back into the veils of Avalon to preserve the teachings of The Way. Others traveled to different lands to seed the message and create memory impressions in and around the land for those who had ears to hear. Avalon, the area that is now Glastonbury was one place, along with Hibernia (Scotland) and Eire (Ireland).

The marriage of the Divine Feminine with the Divine Masculine could only be retained by those who knew the path of the Goddess. To preserve this sacred union, the Way of the Wise Women had to be cloaked and concealed. Look at the harm that was done to women who were not! While many tried to stay out in the open, it was dangerous and deadly. You and others hold those memories of those lifetimes. We share more of this time, with the practices and preaching, so that the memories and matrixes of Light and Love will be remembered. Just allow yourself; many of you can feel it coming.

As Magdalene finished this long addendum about Avalon, I started to realize the enormity of what I was receiving. I also started wondering about the next stages of the book. I loved being in the open expansiveness of the spiritual connection and writing as it flowed. I hungered for more stories and for her wisdom about the Divine Feminine, which I sensed were to come. What next? How to proceed? I wasn't so sure. As always, Magdalene responded to my unspoken thoughts.

Mary Magdalene: It is critical that you review the messages already received. We know you resist. Please come to it in joy, and then you will see gaps and have questions. From there we can elaborate further. There is more to be shared, but this re-orientation must come first, dear. For today, we are complete.

I was moved by the immense beauty of Magdalene's life. I noticed how her story wove a context and created a foundation for her teachings about the Divine Feminine. This was not abstract history (or, as Magdalene says, "herstory") lessons. I saw how they directly related to and impacted our lives as women today.

With her pieces of historical reframing completed, Mary Magdalene was quite clear that my next step was to review and organize the material I'd received. I danced around doing this; it didn't seem as juicy and fun as getting Divine Downloads of "herstory" from a Divine being. I loved the meditation and immersing myself in Spirit energy while writing; it didn't seem like work. I knew that the task of organizing the material was going to require actual focus and effort—hours (months!) of sifting and sorting, adding my perspective, and filling in holes with more messages. I started to sort the writing into chapters that you see here, using the outline I was given in the very beginning. The illumination of the Divine Feminine with rich, inspired guidance for women of our day emerged next.

Temple Garden © 2014 Claire Sierra

Chapter 3

The Path of the Divine Feminine

Encouragement and Guidance

As I received the messages from Mary Magdalene about her life and various untold aspects of "herstory," she started to weave in guidance about the awakening of the Divine Feminine—key concepts, insights, and tools to uplift our consciousness as women. She also continued to convey her support and direction about my life, along with the process of writing the book. Rather than tangle all these Divine Downloads together, I sorted them as Magdalene suggested. After much rearranging, various categories emerged and the chapters coalesced.

As I was sifting through the material, I saw that there was so much more to it than I remembered. It puzzled me that I still struggled sometimes to sustain my enthusiasm, attention, and focus. When I finally sat down for my next meditation, Magdalene addressed this immediately with guidance that could be relevant for you as well:

Mary Magdalene: We understand. That is part of the design of the experience. You do not have full awareness of what you are getting, even though you are completely conscious when you receive these downloads from me. Do not squander your precious life energy on petty concerns or grievances, such as this. Just come back, listen, and start typing. There is much to do.

You are an awakener of the Divine in all, but especially in women, as your "medicine" relates to the Divine Feminine, in female and male forms. The means to do this is not yet clear to you, but through this process with us, you will start to understand. There are practices you teach and share (as well as use daily yourself) that are fundamental to your being. These come from your long lineage with us, as one of us.

These practices and skills are going to become more transparent to you in the weeks and months ahead. You are so busy judging yourself and this process, that the wisdom that is spewing forth is disregarded. Simple wisdom is simple truth. It is still powerful and transformational for others, despite what you think and thus believe otherwise. So while we do appreciate your discernment and sense of quality control, it would be wise for you to let us do the driving while you navigate, as you are so well equipped.

We also understand that you do not believe you have a message, which is simply not true. Your message is not yet refined to a place that you can state it simply, but you have a message, and it will become clear in this process. We feel you have a great deal to say, and this is only the beginning.

We will guide you when you are faltering. Just show up, and we will advise of the next area or topic. Sometimes it will come directly from us, other times it will come out of you as your wisdom becomes clearer. By spending this time with us, you'll get clarity about the message. Perhaps a weekend away would allow you to cloister yourself and focus.

Thinking about this later, I realized that the "design" of this process (as

Magdalene called it) had a striking parallel to the process of writing my Master's Degree thesis in Expressive Arts Therapy. My method then was equally vague, organic, intuitive, unstructured, and at times totally confounding. And that experience had similar frustrations. I didn't have a complete grasp of what I was writing about until it was nearly completed. Yet, in the end, it did come together, though far differently than I had expected. I started to see how that experience had been training for this one. Perhaps this is this how I write and process information? Or was I discovering a Divine Feminine style of literature? I hoped the process would smooth out and become clear soon.

The Practices: A Note

This is the first of many practices that are included in the book, which are intended to guide and support you in connecting more deeply with your Feminine Soul through the Magdalene Path. I invite you to start your exploration with these offerings. Some of these practices come directly from Mary Magdalene's Divine Downloads and others I've used for years in my counseling and coaching work. Still others I developed to enhance your learning experientially, so that you could better integrate this material into your life. While some of us learn best intellectually, it is not until we actually practice something, that the changes become part of our lives.

I've noticed that as I give myself more time for these Soul Care practices in the morning and throughout my day, I am more focused, aligned, centered, present, and alive. I am less inclined to ramp-up old, exhausting habits, which though helpful at times, can also be a draining. I'm less likely to be short-sighted, agitated, ill-tempered or drive myself mercilessly. I connect with Source guidance first and let my Feminine Soul lead. I allow the flow of life, Spirit wisdom, and body-based intuition to guide and direct my day. Then planning and action arise, by first *being* and then *doing*.

The Practice: Feed the Feminine First

Feeding Feminine Soul means taking time and making time for ourselves, every day. Do some kind of Soul Care practice first thing upon waking. This enlivens and enhances the Divine Feminine within. We signal to ourselves and the world that our needs are important and that we can tend them. Notice how much better you feel when you do these practices with some regularity, versus how you feel and how your day unfolds when you skip this morning Soul Care. (Again, don't shoot for perfection!) By starting our day off this way we set a tone and mood that is positively addicting.

1. Choose one Soul Care skill or tool that you can easily and effortlessly slip into your morning routine for 5-10 minutes after you first wake up. This could be meditating or journaling before getting out of bed, saying prayers or setting intentions while in the shower, doing yoga or taking a walk.

   - What practices or activities really support and sustain you?

   - Can you commit to taking 5 or 10 minutes in your morning to do these practices?

2. Don't try to be perfect, just start with 1-3 minutes if 5 is too much!

3. Add and/or increase practices as you are inspired. You will benefit from giving yourself this Soul nourishment each morning. And so will everyone else around you!

Feminine Transformation

I felt curious about what was starting to emerge, and equally curious about how it would all weave together. I loved meditating in the presence of Magdalene; her energy was always focused, clear, light, and lovely. And I loved the different topics she placed before me, winding into areas and themes that I never expected. It was such a ride. I was hopeful and uplifted as the process evolved. When I next sat and centered for *Listening* meditation several days later, Mary Magdalene appeared, easily, as usual.

Mary Magdalene: Today, dear, we wish to speak about the role of the feminine at this time on the planet. There are great changes that are occurring, and even more that need to. The feminine force is a primary tool for this transformation. When we say "feminine," we are not specifically talking about females. Though women are a primary carrier of the feminine energy, you are not the sole component. There are plenty of men who have an awakened awareness of the feminine within themselves, or at least the value and power of it in others.

At this time of great change, there is much that needs to occur. Countless books, articles, and discussions are happening on this topic. What needs to arise is not articulated clearly, but the fact that things must change—this is agreed. A large part of this is already being done by the feminine power or energy which we call Soul.

First, perhaps we should review the energetic of the Divine as feminine and masculine in form. You are well aware, and we have written previously, about power imbalances that began to be created 5,000 years or so ago. While there are opinions about evil entities, dark forces, and conspiracies of control, in actuality much of what came to pass was simply due to fear and ignorance. This was grounded in a firm reality of separation that was emerging.

This disconnect from Source, the power and supply of everything, was a long time in coming. This did not happen overnight or even over the course of a decade. Instead, it was a gradual process, based in fear and the illusion of life not providing enough. This illusion creates fear and hardship along with the belief in the drama of getting one's needs met (or one's family or living community, village or tribe) at the expense of the needs of another individual or group.

The fear and separation—a sense of "not-enough"—allowed a coarseness and mistrust in life to emerge. From there, raiding, looting, killing, and controlling all started to become commonplace. Once set in place, a strong energy to break.

Throughout that time of transition, there were always those who felt violence, anger, and stealing were not the answer. They understood that there were other options, including cooperation or collaboration. They knew that anger, hatred, war, and violence were optional—that sometimes the law of supply and demand (or who has what) cannot be comprehended by those living in the world of third-dimensional reality. They always held the knowledge that good-seeming events can turn out poorly and vice-versa — and that Spirit understood all, regardless.

There has been a constant line, a thread for this past 3,000 years, that is based in the belief that those "in-game" (as we like to call those who are spirit choosing to incarnate in form) are sometime "haves" and sometime "have-nots." They understood that there are blessings to be had by experiencing both. So taking from one to the other is not solving the problem; it only distracts from finding a true Spirit-based solution.

Natural Ebb and Flow

So, imagine in your mind's eye a village, primitive and raw. This could be anywhere during various eras. At times there would be plenty, and the people would rejoice and celebrate. In this celebration, there would be the creation of new life and new community. Eventually the harvest would fail, weather or other misfortune would occur, and the expanded community could not be supported. Some would fall away, going off to another location, hoping for better options and more plenty. Others would become sick and die. The community would therefore naturally contract to course-correct. This was understood as part of the natural cycle of life. Those Souls would see that their time was complete, exiting for others to flourish. There was a natural ebb and flow.

Through the ages, this awareness has become lost. A belief became instilled (encouraged by your dominant religious systems) that evil forces were creating the loss of crops or a sickness that would sweep through a valley or nation. Instead, a balancing of life forms on the planet was actually happening. Humans began forgetting that you are part of that natural cycle of life, subject to the culling of the herd, like other animals and plants in nature.

Part of the challenge your community of humans faces now is that the natural cycle of life is being tampered with to an extreme. Everything is artificially enlarged and enhanced. Even those with so-called spiritual values have forgotten the law of flow, and how in excess there is expansion and in scarce times there is retraction or, to use your local language, recession. This is natural. The lives of those who are born or lost are quite naturally part of and an expression of that cycle.

With advances of modern medicine, farming/agriculture, industrial food production, and global distribution, the challenge is to avoid artificial manipulation of the natural ebb and flow. It is natural to want your loved ones to survive. At first the measures to do so seemed simple, elegant, and not in conflict with the balance of nature. But as culture has progressed and become quite complex, this is changing. Those whose time should be passing are extended somewhat indefinitely. They are defying the laws of nature. This is unpopular to even consider and discuss.

This becomes even further complicated, a paradox, for the Souls on their journey who are here at this time and place are in perfect alignment. They were destined to be born into a technological time and culture where lives could be unnaturally expanded. No one dies before (or after) their time. When the contract for incarnation is complete, it is done. So in another sense it is perfect and in divine right order!

Speak Loudly

Now, here is where the role of the Divine Feminine comes in. It is perfect to accept and allow this flow of natural life force in keeping with one's Soul contract. Many who are in harmony with the natural and spiritual evolution on the planet see, feel, and sense the overburden as it occurs. There is need and a rising movement toward creating balance and harmony regarding the access and distribution of resources.

The task of the feminine is to speak loudly for this balance and care of the planet and all her peoples. It is natural that women, who are more deeply connected to cycles and seasons, lead this call. Women, through the cycles of birth, sex, death, and menstruation—what we call the Blood Mysteries—have an inborn ability. You are intimately aware of the changes that occur in your bodies, as well as those around you. The culture attempts to silence and suffocate this, but a natural inclination or body-based wisdom, causes this awareness in the first place. Who better than women to speak to the damages to the planet and the impact this has on her inhabitants?

While humans are not children, it could be argued that you are acting like spoiled ones. You always want more and rarely appreciate what you have, seeing the basket as empty when it is often full. This is particularly true in Western or industrial cultures, where the mindset of "more, better" is a rampant virus that threatens to overtake all.

So the call is urgent for women and men sensitive to the yearning for balance and respect to heed this plea. Enter into direct dialogue about the need to rethink the power balance as it has been played out. Find those who are ready to listen.

The Practice: Stepping into Feminine Leadership

Are there places in your own life where you feel particularly called — situations or issues that grab your attention? Are you able to speak up with care, concern, and compassion? Often we keep these awarenesses hidden for fear of upsetting the status quo, wanting to keep the peace, etc. Those days need to be over, as we are reaching crises of epic proportions in almost all areas of society.

1. Tune in to your breath, your body and heart. Let your mind settle down. Breathe deeply and slowly.

2. Ask your heart: Are there any key issues or areas you are concerned about? (You may not need to ask, or you might see pictures appear in your heart-mind.) Journal about what comes up for you. Be careful not to judge, just be curious.

3. Keep breathing. This slows everything down.

4. Are there any areas of your life: your community, family, town, or church, where you feel you could make more impact?

5. What areas, issues, or interests could you become more engaged and outspoken about?

6. Is there one action, one issue you could give voice to? You could take one small step, like making a phone call, sitting in on a meeting you wouldn't usually go to (but would like to), or speaking up in a controversial conversation when you might normally stay quiet. Ask your body wisdom, inner knowing, heart, or Source how to best respond. (Or who/whatever you feel connected to.)

    - Could you do that this week or this month? Make it a small step, if it is particularly sensitive and triggering.

7. As women we thrive in working together, yet we often feel isolated. We don't have to do it alone anymore. What can you do to get support? Can you get your community involved with you?

8. Appreciate yourself for your care and concern, for being willing to be willing. You don't need to have an answer or plan, and this in and of itself can be uncomfortable.

9. Journal your thoughts, feelings, and intuitions. By listening to your instinct, you activate your intuitive wisdom. It will get louder when heeded. Writing down these "hits" helps immensely. Otherwise, this guidance is easy to overlook or discount.

God, Goddess, and All There Is

I thought a lot about the importance about all this Goddess business for many days. I hesitated to get aligned with a "movement" to awaken this Divine Feminine, because I felt that *everything* is "Godstuff." Source or Spirit—the Divine creative force—is genderless, and I didn't want be part of creating more male/female, "us and them" polarity in the world. God/Goddess is embodied in all kinds of sacred form: people, animals, plants, nature. All living things are created by this Spirit and often have a gender. But everything, in essence, still is all One, all God. I brought these thoughts to Magdalene, and was interested in how she'd respond.

Mary Magdalene: One aspect we want to emphasize is that the expression or awakening of the Goddess IS happening. For many this is a good entry point—to see, feel, connect, and relate to an aspect of the Divine in female form that was worshipped for millennia. "Goddessing" is a very viable access point for many women to relate to.

Ultimately we agree. The Divine is awakening in all, and we do not wish to encourage more separation among you. No feuding God/Goddess wars. The Divine in all is awakening, you are correct. That is a mystery play that is being spun right before your eyes. In the awakening, men need to own their divinity, too. The God of your Abrahamic religions may be male in gender, but he is not "one of the guys" for your male partners to relate to. As a result, since God is outside of and above them, they model themselves after a deity that is distant, aloof, and judging.

However the "New Age" (and other philosophies) also fail by conspiring to create a gender-neutral form of divinity. By identifying the Divine as "the Universe," Source remains outside of you, infinite and impersonal, not related and embodied. It is not connected to creating in Godhood on Earth. It is a large swirl of galaxy: large, expansive, and all-encompassing, like the external father God in the sky many were raised with. This aspect of divinity remains separate and distant, much like the God of your ancestors (Yahweh, Allah, Jehovah, and perhaps even Jesus)—Divine Beings that are outside of you, separate and complete.

In reality, God (or Goddess, your preference) is in everything and everyone. Your people are not aware of that yet, but you are becoming more so. The perspective of New Thought teachings comes closer to this reality. That philosophy teaches the awareness that we are all one part of God, that you are in and of God. You are an aspect of the Divine living into human form. There are other religions and esoteric streams within the major religions, which have had this perspective. But because it is so radically self-referencing and intangible, it has been written out of or conveniently ignored in the great books.

The belief has been that as long as God is outside of you, you need to go to a "God-connector" (priest, rabbi, imam, guru, etc.). When God is within, there is no longer a need for that hierarchy as a point of connection. The perceived threat to the religious hierarchy is that the spiritual leaders would no longer be needed, although that is false.

People always need community and focus for worship, along with education. Everyone needs guidance and support for realignment with God and Truth when life naturally causes us to forget. Your forgetting would be lessened with *the inborn knowledge and teaching from birth that we are all God. You are social creatures. You are not meant to do it alone, just as you seek support from spiritual guides and mentors now. There is still need for community and congregation is a natural expression, but not from a place of coercion or fear.*

The Practice: Goddessing

I like using *Goddess* as a verb. When we are *Goddessing*, we tap in to our Divine nature. It's an intrinsic art of Feminine Soul magic to connect to our Goddess selves and live from this awareness. We can embody our higher selves and access our essence in this way. This meditation and body prayer practice starts to activate your Divine Feminine. Take 5 or 10 minutes daily (or more if you desire) to connect with your Self as a Divine being and see how your inner and outer world start to change. As I've engaged this practice, I've noticed a big shift.

1. Start by creating sacred space for yourself. Turn off your phone, close your door, light a candle, and play some sweet, inspiring music.

2. Close your eyes and breathe deeply to relax and center yourself for a few moments.

3. Imagine yourself in an exquisite garden, forest grove, or other naturally sacred space.

4. Notice a path and a beautiful temple, luminously lit from within. Travel down the path, toward the temple. When you arrive, the doors open. Notice all you see, feel, sense, and imagine. (If you see nothing, don't worry, just continue.)

5. Call in your Divine Feminine Essence. Ask her to show herself to you, in your mind's eye or your heart. Feel, sense, or imagine her before you. (Allow yourself to be surprised.) Greet her. Receive the blessings she is here to bring you today. Spend time being with her in silence, or imagine talking with her if you like.

6. Allow her to move into you, fusing her energy body with yours. Feel her radiant, sensuous essence. Let it shine throughout your body. Imagine it radiating out into the world.

7. Allow your connection to Her energy in your body to move in ways that feel easy and delicious. Know that she and you are one. Breathe.

8. After a few minutes, when your time feels complete, say thank you to Her. Know you can return to Her any time you need guidance or an infusion of this energy.

9. Journal or create art about your experiences. Even potent, powerful visions or messages tend to fade quickly and may be lost if not written down.

10. While it is helpful to do this intentionally in the morning (or evening if you prefer), the full practice of Goddessing is to weave this into your day. For brief moments, allow yourself to call up an image, feeling, or body-based sensation of your full Divine Feminine self. Shine this essence out to those around you as you move through your life. As you remember this practice, you can speak, move, and live from this radiant place.

*If you'd like to be led in this meditation and body prayer, go to MagdalenePath.com for a free downloadable audio recording of this practice in the Free Resources section of the website.

Compass Point of Purpose

One morning, I noticed that I was feeling "off"—at odds with myself, my life. Nothing was particularly wrong, but I felt slightly off-course. That's usually a sign that there's guidance I wasn't heeding or a deeper layer was ready to come to me. I decided to lay it at the metaphorical feet of the Magdalene, to see what her perspective was. As I settled into my seat with my warm tea nearby, I started to type my concerns. Magdalene came immediately into my meditation and soon we were off and running.

Claire: I'm feeling lost again and frustrated that I don't know what I should be doing with my life, and what my purpose is. Yet I realize, I do know. This project is my purpose. And my malaise is related to my not doing the review and sorting that you suggested I do next. Is that right? Is there more?

Mary Magdalene: Greetings, we wish you no remorse for not completing our suggested task. The next phase will be reviewing and sorting this into a cogent and coherent piece of writing that can be disseminated to the masses. This can be accomplished while away on your upcoming retreat and renewal trip. We look forward to the excitement and clarity of purpose we know you will feel when you begin to grasp the elegance and artistry that is here within. This is a clear, beautiful piece of writing, and though we know you do not always see it as such, we hope that this will be conveyed to you soon.

Today we would like to speak about the awakening of the Divine Feminine and your role in this project. First, we would encourage you to relax. There is really not much difference in what you are going to be offering, although your framework will be altered dramatically by the awareness you will hold in your consciousness about what you do and why you are doing it.

Previously, you were aware that your mission and blessing (your unique purpose and specific gifts) were in service to the awakening of the Divine in all. This is still true. We point you to be particularly attuned to the realm of the awakening feminine, for in this matter you are complete.

The primary task before you is to remember always that this is your purpose. So use this as a compass point. Whenever you are speaking to someone, even casually, or thinking about a new project or next direction, you must ask yourself, "Is this in service to the awakening of the Feminine Divine?" In this way, the frame you hold for yourself and your work can be varied yet consistent. This is the new compass (or litmus test) for "purposefulness" that we wish for you to incorporate. It is from you holding the space for the importance of this task that you will become a messenger.

Immediately upon receipt of this message, I felt myself relax. I still didn't know exactly what my message or method was, yet I felt unusually buoyant from this inspiration and direction. I liked having something clear to focus on and the "litmus test for purposefulness" to keep me on track when I got distracted.

Message to Share

Mary Magdalene: This is the message we wish for you to share: For too long, the feminine has been denied and repressed: from religion, politics, and many areas of society. Women have learned how to use this and work around it. Some things have changed, but there are certain assumptions that have not. Just notice the imbalance that still exists in levels of power in business, religion, government, etc. Though there is a "feeling" of equality among many, it has not played out in full expression within mainstream culture yet.

As a result, there are choices being made that do not take in the full range of decision-making for women. The feminine (in either gender) is not being accounted or spoken for. There is a new way of thinking and being that is emerging. And, while we do not have full access to this yet, we are in the process of waking it up in each of us.

This is happening in men as well as women, for the method and style of the Divine Masculine is awakening as well. The controlling, imbalanced masculine is not a full expression of the male in his most Divine and expressed form. The world still needs the masculine mode, there is no denying this. We are looking toward a time when both male and female, masculine and feminine, are held and honored for equal but different styles, tasks, and ways of being.

As we come into balance between the gender split, we will have more of a sense of wholeness and androgyny. The full acceptance and receipt of what has been hidden, denied, and repressed for so long is massively important. Because the sacred feminine has been hidden (stuffed down, really), it has been forgotten. This is the feminine face of God, expressed in the humanity of female—though not only in women, for the feminine aspect exists in each of us. You each hold the polarity of male and female, some in greater or lesser degrees, but in polarity nonetheless.

As the Divine in feminine form is respected as sacred, these qualities will naturally come to be expressed in men and women alike. For the fear of that which has been beaten back in each of us will come to the fore and easily flow forth.

This is the time on your lovely planet home to bring the balance and harmony back. You (and many like you) are players in this game. It is a shared vision and mission. As you develop your clear, strong voice of light and hope, you will draw to you others that have similar vision. And they will be drawn to you.

For now, be content to continue here. For we are not yet complete, this project will continue. You will have much to do and much help to do it, so do not be afraid.

I was excited to get a direct transmission of my message, but I admit that the wording seemed a bit esoteric. I hoped it would become clearer and more everyday-relatable. My concerns were lessened as I shared snippets (cautiously) with others; they seemed intrigued, awestruck, and impressed. This boosted my confidence in the potential of what was happening here and how it could positively impact others.

The Practice: Align from Your Purpose

Here is a decision-making tool to orient your daily activities as well as your life goals. What are your primary goals or guidelines for your life? This simple process allows you to develop your internal compass or litmus test of purpose.

As I became clear about my core values and started aligning my decision-making from my purpose, my outer reality started to change. Decision making, daily planning, and life choices became simpler (but not always easy) by just asking these key questions. The activities, people, and things that were not in alignment with my purpose started to become very obvious and fall away. Sometimes there was purposeful action on my part, which was coincidentally met with other non-aligned things being removed from my path.

1. Write down 3-5 values or interests that you organize your life around, that feel positive and affirming. Notice whether they are self-determined or societally imposed.

2. Choose, or ask for guidance to be shown, the one value most in alignment with your Soul Contract. If nothing comes, use the values developed above. It helps to write it down for reference.

3. Develop intentions for your week or season based from these. This points you toward your purpose.

4. Then develop goals from there, which can manifest into daily activities and plans.

5. As you move through your day, orient your choices, preferences, and habits around what you understand as your purpose (however vague or specific it may be).

6. When confronted with decisions and choices in your life, ask yourself, "Is this (insert decision here) in alignment with my purpose to (insert value here)?" or "Is this helping me to fulfill my life-intention to live a life of (insert value)?"

7. Journal your thoughts and feelings.

Collaboration with Spirit

I was moving forward and felt jazzed about the way the material was pouring through me and coming together. With that, Magdalene shared some new guidance and direction for healing:

Mary Magdalene: We can begin to discuss the new healing model or modality that the team alluded to previously. Your current process for coaching and counseling is too confining and structured, too flat and rigid. It is smooth, straight, and bland, like your drywall. There is another way, and it is one you know well in your Soul, but has no name or "system," so it is far more difficult to pin down. Your present style allows for this, when you do not rigidly adhere to someone else's rules or steps. This is a shift from the masculine to the feminine mode of healing.

Instead, focus on creating a container, a series of experiences that would facilitate access to Divine connection. Allow yourself to develop partnership and collaboration with Spirit allies, rather than obedience and worship. That is a fine model, but it's just not what we are advising here.

The path of obedience and worship has served humanity well for thousands of years, when Spirit was not understood and superstition was rampant. Now that we are on the brink of an evolutionary leap, the physics of Spirit into form is far more easily grasped. Therefore, a method of blind, unquestioning obedience is not as relevant in your culture. Though it still exists and does serve a portion of your population, it is not the wave of the future.

Instead, you are at the crest of a wave that has to do with the various forms of relationship with Spirit that is relational and connected. Counsel and collaboration are names for this. You can be in direct partnership with the Divine in order to get messages that are specific, practical, and timely for decisions you need to make.

You are aware of this and are destined to teach this to large groups. We know you do not see this or believe us. Trust us in the knowledge we see in the Akashic Records—that great collective unconscious library of all history—and what it holds for you.

So there is a method of relating to Spirit (or God or Source, whichever you prefer) that allows individuals the freedom to choose, and yet be open to advice. This way is clean, clear, and direct, from Source to you. Then you choose. We do not advise blind faith, only that you ask and receive the guidance, then act according to your best intentions, choices, values, and resources.

This is a model that also enhances the awareness of the feminine face of God. We could call this Goddess, but do not. We know the trigger for many who resist that turn of phrase. So we say Divine Feminine, and trust you know what we mean.

We are not encouraging you to focus solely on women, for men need the Divine Feminine far more than most realize. Some would argue that they need it more! In truth, you both do, but in different ways. So this path is expressed as engagement with the Divine, in partnership versus worship, while activating the feminine face of God.

It is not a complete picture, but a good catch for today. Start with this and chew on it a bit. Thank you for letting us in and letting us know your time and energy commitment, as that makes our work that much easier. We love you and believe we are complete for tonight.

I felt satiated by this guidance and direction, like after eating a delicious feast. Of course I have questions about how it will play out, but I felt really complete inside.

Clever Play

With all that was happening as the process unfolded, I felt more consistent and inspired by the material that was coming to me. The process was carrying me—finally! I started to feel the message in my body, not just in my mind. I used the Divine Feminine as a compass point, to align me in my daily decision-making and business direction. This felt collaborative and inspired—I wasn't at the mercy of some grand God being, but guided and coached in ways that empowered me. It felt real and supportive. Several days passed, and I sat down again to talk (and listen) to Magdalene. What she shared emerged as a core message with enormous personal and collective ramifications.

Claire: Okay, so what is my next step? I wonder if there is any input or upgrades from last week.

Mary Magdalene: It is good to have you in the process of relationship with us. This is the Divine Feminine at work. You are right in your observation and assumption that the loss of the feminine aspect of Divine, in the forms of worship and deity, has been a great loss to your culture as a whole and the planet at large.

There is more to this than meets the eye. It is not merely that the women are left out, or that you do not have an image or essence to worship that is similar to and reflects your female form. Yes, these are painful and detrimental, but not in the ways you suspect. Certainly, there is a great loss for women in eons of spiritual worship of only a male God. The inner meaning is clear: You are not Divine.

The message given was that all humans are made in the image and likeness of God. This would imply genderless or dual-gendered deity. Therefore, if you are made in the image of God, and you are female, then God must be female, also. Somehow this logic leap did not breach the gap of awareness. Instead, the idea was passed down that God is male. And since human men are made in the image and likeness of God, they are therefore more Divine. (Actually all creation is, not just humanity, but that larger misinterpretation is best left for another time.) For centuries, this was bought and sold as Truth. Such folly.

This was a clever power play at the hands of those who wished to maintain control. It was a strategy more about acquisition of power and property than ideology or theology. There is no basis in fact that women have no Souls (as was long taught), and yet after that is woven into consciousness year after year for centuries, the absence of fact goes unnoticed. So this creates a thought-field, which is critical to undo, for it has informed the consciousness of your land for quite some time.

Great Loss

We find what emerges from this thought-form is even more relevant. With the loss of the Divine Feminine, the Divine Masculine lost his partner/consort. He lost his balance and his Self in the Divine deism of the day. This loss of partnership is reflected in how hyper-masculinized your culture has become. The qualities of the over-amped masculine: straight, rigid, planned, controlled, and organized, have become the highlight of society. They became the great endpoint and goal to be striving toward.

Now, we acknowledge that there is great value in those qualities, but understand they are not the only ones. Their companion, opposite in the spectrum, has been devalued and discounted. The feminine qualities of being spontaneous, organic, intuitive, unpredictable, emotional, eclectic have become denounced as disorganized, chaotic, or uncontrolled. They have been hailed as diseases to be cured from and have been avoided at all cost, at times. All manner of projects and programs are directed at eliminating the latter (the feminine) to the elevation and worship of the former (the masculine).

As a result, there is hardly room for those qualities to be valued and cultivated. Yet they are great creation tools, too, just a different form and style. Not better, not worse, just different. These feminine qualities come from a more grounded embodied place of being, rather than intellect and doing. This capacity of the driving doer is seen as "better" than the quality of the receptive meanderer, which is intrinsically a set up against the feminine ways of being.

There is more we could say here, but will address it later. Suffice to say this awareness — that the feminine creates differently in style and process — is huge and not to be overlooked. Even as you engage with us, notice how your habit is to plan. Instead, be present in the process (as we have suggested from the outset) which allows it unfold, like meandering down the path. Be in the process, attempt to resist controlling, and watch it develop right before your eyes, even without a plan. Imagine that!

Reclaim the Sacred Self

Mary Magdalene: A woman with a reclaimed Divine inner Feminine has a sense of herself as whole and holy. She is held by God and knows that, since she is part of and connected to Source, she is Sacred. As a result, she is not willing to abuse or abandon herself in any of the myriad ways women do.

Claire: We can care without caretaking. We can love without codependency. We can relax without numbing. We can relate without giving ourselves away.

Mary Magdalene: This is why it such deep and important work. Women are now ready to reveal their true divinity to themselves and the world. And the world needs all the self-expressed, inspired, confident, love-blazed women ready to live as a force to be reckoned with. Not out of anger or aggression, but a fierce, vibrant force of love, like a strong breeze at the end of a long, hot summer day. The world needs this wind of change and the cleansing force it implies. Be ready; the wind is coming your way. Trust your voice, your skills, your inspiration and intuition. They are not off, and it is time.

Claire: Blessed be. I bow in gratitude and thanks.

I reflected on this writing later that night, and went to bed feeling fulfilled and uplifted. I felt good that I was following through on my guidance to be in the project in this manner. The process and the message were beginning to make sense to me. I was excited to see it unfolding (as Magdalene said it would), right before my eyes!

The Practice: Living from Being

Notice, in your own life, when you undertake a project or plan your day, how your primary process may be to plan, organize, and control. This is habit and conditioning from society. Yet by being in the Divine Feminine energy field, you can start to let your project, day, or life unfold organically, as if you were meandering down a path. By being in the flow of your life, resisting control and not forcing outcome, you will watch your ideas and intentions develop right before your eyes, even without a conscious plan. Imagine that!

This practice awakens awareness of patterns and habits so that you can start to make other choices and shift your being. You will evoke a deeper listening to connect to your inner wisdom, also called intuition or "the still small voice within." This is an initial step towards your own *Listening.*

1. Give yourself extra time in the morning to attend to your Divine Feminine self with soul-care and spiritual practices. These will support and sustain you, allowing your Feminine Essence to shine into your day. Starting off with rules, structure, and discipline may get things done, but at a big cost to your true

vitality and radiance. You may be uploading some cultural programming, restricting a deeper, juicier connection to your Feminine Soul.

- What practices or activities really support and sustain you?
- Give yourself 5 or 10 minutes in your day morning for these practices, to start you day in connection with your Essence.

2. Now, as you start your day faced with an outer request or need, tune in deeply to what you feel called to do. Place your hand on your heart and take a full, deep, slow breath. You don't need to have an answer or plan right away (this can be uncomfortable).

3. Start by taking a few minutes to journal about your thoughts, feelings, and intuitions. By paying attention to your deeper instinct, you activate your intuitive wisdom. It will get louder when heeded. Writing down these "hits" helps immensely. Otherwise, this guidance is easy to overlook or discount.

4. Breathe deeply and slowly. This slows everything down.

5. Ask your body wisdom, inner knowing, heart, or Source how to best respond. (You may call this Goddess, Mary Magdalene, Spirit, Jesus, or whatever you feel connected to.)

6. More breathing.

7. Jot down your thoughts, feelings, perceptions, questions, and answers. You may not get the reactive answer or action you might normally. The messages will get clearer or stronger as you attend to them — and dry up if you continue to ignore them. All skills get refined when practiced, and your feminine guidance is among them.

8. Give thanks for the guidance you have received, from whatever Source it came from.

Awaken the Divine Feminine

Claire: Is there a short piece of wisdom that I can start with now? My time management got away from me. I need to get ready and leave for an appointment in 20 minutes.

Mary Magdalene: We wish to share the critical pieces for you in the movement to awaken the Divine Feminine.

Feed the feminine first. Cultivate feminine essence in all you do and be. Create a daily practice and engage it as a priority. Make time for Soul with self-care and connection every day, to draw in a stronger awareness and experience of the Feminine Soul.

Realize she is already within you. *The feminine is alive. She has endured, dormant and hidden for many generations. In your land, the awakening began through a politico-social process with the 1960's and 1970's "women's liberation" movement. This, in fact, began at the turn of the last century, and culminated in 1920 as women engaged the right to vote. How absurd that half the population did not have rights to give voice in the government, societal, or political landscape. It seems impossible now, though there are still lands where women have little if no freedom. And so, as the feminine fully awakens in a social and spiritual dimension, the Divine partnership will be recognized in religious and cultural landscapes. This, too, will one day seem impossible.*

Know that women are God, too. *What you are awakening is the recognition of the absolutely inherently spiritual and soulful aspect of women. The group that is awakening is now coming to the awareness that there is not a male God governing over all. That would be an extreme version of self-consciousness and grandiosity, to think that one gender would have more access to the spiritual dimension than another. But, for generations and centuries, this was the official story. There was a time when the belief was you believed that women* had no Soul, and with no connection to God needed access through men. That is ultimate power in patriarchy, for when one controls the inner dimension, the outer aligns quickly.

Men are not the problem, nor the solution. Males in your culture are just as controlled and negatively impacted by patriarchal conditioning as women. Their expression as Spirit beings has been limited, too. They are in a tighter box than women, albeit holding the reins of power.

The uprising Feminine Soul is a wave of creation and expression. Speak about this to all you see and know. As you do, these ideas and concepts will incubate and develop. It is the sacred exchange of the creative self in art, movement, dance, music, and word play that enables more to flow. Begin this articulation. Start the shift in awareness. Later lessons will emerge clearly as you get deeper into this body of work. (Yes, that is a pun.)

The means becomes the end. As you express the sacredness of your feminine form, you will move with Spirit and experience your being, your Self as Divine. Then recognize the Divine in all. Such is the ultimate goal: to recognize your Godhood, your Goddess self, in physical form. You are all creatures of God/Goddess, and it is time for your awakening to occur. But first, at least half the population needs to awaken, to acknowledge and experience a change in consciousness about the packaging that God comes in. This is a deep psychological shift, and a turn in the psyche is required.

This is a spiritual and a social revolution. It comes from within. Begin to name, experience, and express the feminine essence as Divine. This is still a radical act in many places, even in your environment. There are those who may resist, and they will look away. It is those who move toward you who should be engaged. Let the others fall away, without distaste or ill regard. They have other paths to follow and all is in Divine right order. Trust that.

End the Divine Divorce. *With the glorification of the feminine, the male God is reunited with his female Goddess as partner, co-creator (or creatrix), and consort. It is time for the Divine Union to lead the people and heal the land.*

That is all for now, we will share more later.

Claim the Feminine Face of God

As I received these downloads, I recognized (ironically) how I suppressed my own innate feminine nature. As part of my upbringing and initiation in this culture, raised in the second wave of feminism, that seems unavoidable. Perhaps this is why I was receiving these teachings. In order to be successful, following the model I was raised in, I developed a strong, achievement-oriented, masculinized self. I know I am not unique here. Women have been trained to "man up" in order to compete and succeed in a "man's world." And those roots are many centuries old.

Playing by the rules of the dominant male culture has some benefits for women, certainly. We have more safety, power, and privilege than we've known for eons. But it comes with serious side effects: isolation, irritability, confusion, sadness, and despair. At times, this leads to depression, anxiety, and addiction and a host of other ills. Ultimately, these are symptoms of disconnection from self and Source—not a unique story, and one that is wreaking havoc throughout our world.

Modern women learn early on to keep the "messy" aspects of femininity under wraps. Our emotions, should they spill out, get squashed and apologies ensue. We fear being seen as "too much," while struggling with feeling "not enough." We've been trained to be logical, organized, linear, and practical. These are fantastic traits, but left-brain, masculine qualities are a limited toolkit—especially when it comes to matters of the heart. We've disowned our greatest gifts, and in doing so we've put our lives (and our planet) in peril.

It is time to claim the feminine face of God as Self. I've had to rearrange my psyche to lean into the organic, intuitive, and softer sides of myself, to embrace my Feminine Soul. As you've read, it hasn't always been easy. My masculine doer/achiever self likes being in control. But there is a shift from *doing* to *being* that leads to radiance, aliveness, and vitality. It is emphatically worth the journey. More and more women are profoundly drawn to live from their authentic self, to discover a different, deeper way of being that is more Soul- aligned—even if we don't know how or what that might be.

This shift is often coupled with an increased sense of urgency about how to contribute to life on our lovely garden planet. With near-crisis states of affairs facing us in all areas of society, it seems timely and connected. We are coming to a tipping point. The moment is ripe to weave and repair the relationship with our masculine and feminine sides, both internally and externally. We are called to live a deeper purpose for our lives, in balance and wholeness. The old toolkit is not providing fulfilling solutions.

The collaborative, intuitive, co-creative feminine essence is the perfect antidote, rebalancing humankind toward transformation. We are in great uncharted territory, as the Divine Feminine arises uniquely in each of us. This great blossoming is a revelation into outer, structural changes that would otherwise overwhelm us. We receive inspired solutions that are needed for a world torn apart. As we reclaim and own our God/Goddess identity, we infuse new possibility into our lives and those around us.

Divine Union © 2014 Claire Sierra

Chapter 4

Sacred Partnership

Early on in recorded history, most women absorbed the cultural and religious messages of male dominance as status quo. We've worked hard for decades to undo that. To prove ourselves worthy and equal, women have adopted values, attitudes, and behavior that are essentially masculine. We've become mini-men, working harder, faster, and stronger to succeed. As successful as this strategy is, it's also a recipe for exhaustion and burnout, not to mention chronic stress, adrenal fatigue, and other ills.

It is no longer productive or healthy to fight to be treated like men in order to be heard or respected. Women bear different gifts and talents. It's time for our instinctive, *feminine* voice and vision to emerge, to stand as full partners in the world dialogue. This begs the question: What is the Feminine, in and of herself? Who are women when we stop modeling ourselves after these largely male traits? The fierce feminine warrioress is an important archetypal energy to connect with. But let's not limit ourselves here. We must seek a deeper, broader, more inclusive vision. What are intrinsic feminine values, psychology, actions, and attitudes?

As we discover, embrace, and express feminine essence in partnership with the values and qualities of the masculine, we are no longer confined by the masculine. We reorient the archetypal elements of Divine She and Divine He – God/Goddess within ourselves, as well as with others. A potent redefining occurs that is not about relationship or romance, per se. (Though that may result.) The time has come to reweave the sacred web of Feminine Soul, to balance and re-pair with the Sacred Masculine. As we do, a co-creative, collaborative Divine partnership emerges.

End the Divine Divorce

One morning, in that liminal space between sleeping and waking, I heard in my mind, "It's time to end the Divine Divorce." As I contemplated this, I imagined it meant that by awakening the Divine Feminine we bring back the Goddess to God, the Holy Bride to the Bridegroom, and reunify the divine couple. I got a glimmering sense of how that could impact humanity, but it was also unclear.

I brewed a strong cup of chai, my favorite wintertime tea, and cozied into a chair in my bedroom alcove. The morning light was lovely. On those dark Pacific Northwest mornings, I gravitated toward all the brightness I could find. As I settled in to my meditation, I felt lightness and calm come over me. After some time in silence, I called to Magdalene for our dialogue. This was her response:

Mary Magdalene: Greetings. We are delighted to meet with you. We have so much in store and are so excited to share it! We encourage you to continue to show up and see what emerges. We are assuming you are aware that there are big changes ahead, not just for you but for many in your population centers. Not that we wish to scare you with thoughts of disasters, for we see greatness happening.

You were hearing us this morning when you realized that "it is time for the Divine Divorce to end." God and Goddess need to be reunited. For many eons the professed "version" of Spirit that predominated in consciousness has been that of the Father God. This was not the case in earlier Egyptian, Greek, or Roman eras, though even in those pantheistic cultures they, too, shifted through time to highlight the Gods while minimizing the Goddesses. Times were changing. With the emergence of the Abrahamic religions (beginning with Judaism, then Christianity and Islam) the role of the male has predominated in the oral and written history.

We have elaborated previously on how and why this occurred. While it was all in the plan to eventually become re-balanced, it was never anticipated to take so long and for so much death, mayhem, and despair to occur in the meanwhile. Your Bibles and sacred texts all speak volumes about the male God with his sons of various forms and faith. These are all good and true. As we have said, what is omitted is the female face of the Godhead, the Mother God.

Without the balance of the masculine and feminine, one form overtakes the whole and the power is off. As Father God is worshipped and Mother God forgotten, the essential yin-yang balance is askew and hierarchy is the result. This has evolved to nations and governments ruling strongly from the masculine, without consultation or partnership with the feminine.

Outer Reflects Inner

This is not only an outward process. It occurs on the inner levels too, as one balances the masculine and feminine aspects within one's own being. While each person has a gender, the fact that one is male does not mean that one has no feminine traits, or that they personify full masculinity. And the opposite is true as well. There are many who are one gender outwardly, yet the opposite gender is dominant internally. Each would benefit from the balance so that one does not have to be so off-kilter.

So we encourage you to write more about the re-union of the masculine and feminine of God, the rebalance that leads to wholeness—the ending of the Divine Divorce.

As I reflected on this message, I couldn't help but notice how this was playing out all around me: in national politics, the environmental and lifestyle choices we make, even at the social and leadership levels in our local communities. Could it really be that all the secular issues we face come from this inner mis-alignment, orienting towards the masculine God and denial of the feminine Goddess? Has this altered our internal self-knowing, resulting in generations of imbalance, low self-esteem, and abuse?

Somehow, there needs to be a shift so that women can embrace this Divine Self and honor the feminine, in balance with the masculine. Ours is a different dance. We can embody the fullness of our Feminine Soul and voice a new vision of a whole, verdant, abundant, harmonious new Earth. How amazing that would be!

The Practice: Defining Feminine and Masculine

Many women find that, due to cultural conditioning and values, we habitually and unconsciously act from a masculine mode of being. Most of the time, we are not even aware of it. We are not acting from our true essence as women. It is not serving us personally or collectively. While this may not be your experience, see if it is. This activity gets you in touch with the dominant masculine and feminine traits and your association to each.

I've been surprised to discover how much I operated from the "masculine" qualities. How habitual and idealized they really are. I also noticed I had more "feminine" qualities than I expected. I was drawn to cultivate them. From this awareness, I began to make conscious choices, at times leaning on one side of the list more than the other. Both are valuable and powerful, and it is important to balance your skills set with non-dominant traits.

1. Make 2 columns, titled "Masculine" and "Feminine," to create lists of qualities.

2. Here are some ideas to get you started. Add and rearrange to your preference.

    Feminine: sensual, chaotic, eclectic, spontaneous, intuitive, emotional

    Masculine: logical, straightforward, assertive, organized, rigid, rational

3. Notice which side you tend to operate from—with no blame, shame, or judgment implied. Journal about your observations.

4. Sense what each list of qualities feels like in your body. What are your feelings about qualities of the other side of the list? What automatic reactions do you have? Really let yourself sink into the essence of each.

5. Move your body or take the posture of each quality on the 2 lists.

6. Using whatever art materials you have handy, image the essence of each list. (Even a basic pen or crayons will do. Just do it.)

7. What thoughts and feelings come up for you? Is one list easier to express than the other?

8. Notice where and when you automatically act from qualities on the lists. What/who is this serving? Know that these are habits and conditioning that can be shifted with attention and care.

9. Journal, paint, draw, or write a poem about your observations.

10. As you move through your life, allow yourself to consciously explore and express qualities from your non-dominant, least-favored list. Be curious about the value in operating from the unexpressed qualities that are embedded in this list.

Recreating Sacred Union

I was thinking about this idea of "ending the Divine Divorce." As I get further into the awakening Divine Feminine, I saw how pervasive this shift can be and how it can impact our relationships. How do we create Sacred Union and equality between the sexes, given the Divine power imbalance that's happening globally? These were my thoughts as I settled in for meditation, centering, and relaxing myself, to receive the wisdom of Magdalene.

Claire: And so what shall we focus on today?

Mary Magdalene: You are right in the midst of big awareness about the emergence of the Divine Feminine and how it relates to the uncovering of the Sacred Union. The awakening of the Divine Masculine will show up in the shadow, the tail of the Feminine. Women need to find the way and guide men by your own example.

The women need to actually surrender more. And this may be hard for you to hear. Surrender here does not mean giving up, or acquiescing as a military conquest. It means allowing without force, giving yourself over to something bigger. In doing so, the Divine Feminine will arise in you and the Divine Masculine will arise in your men. Right now, women are so defended, so strong, independent and capable. You are all quite good at being "mini men." This has been an important developmental leap for you, after eons of repression and misguided information about "the weaker sex." Women needed to rise above that and find a better, stronger way. And there has been benefit, personally and societally. But it has largely been a masculine way —with negative consequences for you and your world, as we have discussed.

In the meantime, paradoxically, men have become out of control on an outward societal level, leading all business, government, and religious structures. But inwardly they have become weak. They are strong in the world to counterbalance the weakness they feel inside and at home with their beloved mates. Women, on the other hand, feel overpowered in the world from the dominance and hierarchy. So how you counterbalance is to be strong at home. Neither gender wants to give up their place of power, for the feeling of weakness is so vulnerable and debilitating.

Holy Other, Holy Self

There is another aspect to the loss of the Divine Feminine, as it relates to partnership. That is, without the sacred balance of the consort, the masculine becomes lonely, creating and destroying wantonly in order to fill that gap. The expressive masculine is looking for the containment of the receptive feminine. In the paired aspect of divinity, we learn how to relate to each other as Divine and holy. If one is led to believe in herself as unholy and impure, the impact and repercussions are dire.

Domestic violence is an aspect of this distortion of reality. Those who know themselves to be Divine would never tolerate abuse. Plus, when you know your partner is sacred, you treat her or him with holy respect. When the feminine was lost in the imbalance of partnership, the masculine God became externalized and open to abuses of power.

As long as God is outside of us, all is lost, for you lose the ability to partner with the immanent aspects of life and Source. When the ability to partner with Spirit is lost, you lose the ability to partner with each other — or with yourself, which is even more dangerous. You become a house divided, with no awareness and no hope of it being any different than it is.

So for women, reclaiming the Sacred Feminine is to remember the sacred in and as yourself. From divided to Divine. From this place, sacred partnerships can be repaired and restored in marriage, friendship, business, and community. Even more importantly, this can begin to happen within.

Healing Gender Dynamics

As you reclaim and own your wholeness, your beloveds, your mates, will in fact blossom as you support their strengths rather than address and berate their weaknesses. This is a reactive habit of disempowerment for many of you. Criticism, even when constructive, does not allow delivery of the intended message. When you criticize, his soft underbelly becomes exposed. Do not poke there! Instead build him up. Allow his strength to carry you, rather than using your own will to control him.

When your men are never allowed to be right, it creates a pattern of failure and dejection, and he feels there is no point in trying. And yet men still keep trying to please women! The Divine quality of the masculine is that they still try to serve, please, and protect, despite the fact that you women are often unpleasable. Once grounded in your own immanent worth and value you can allow and receive the gifts of the men in your life. This cycle of giving and receiving will make you whole.

Avoid the urge to micro-manage. This is a major undermining pattern that women partake in. As women have adopted the strong stance of the masculine culture, some men have never had to take control and step forward, because they know you women will. They feel that if they do, it won't be right (because you are unpleasable), and hence they are afraid to try.

So recognize and appreciate their offerings always, even when they are not as you wish them to be. It is not about molding them to your image and likeness. Or vice versa. Men are not hairy women. They are as God made them, already perfect and complete. See them as such and they will become even more magnificent than you imagine them.

Passion, Sensuality and Creativity

Begin to work within your own life, your own inner and outer marriage. This is a powerful awareness for you to embody. Ultimately that is the task: The inner must balance the outer. The inner marriage is a key to awakening your passion and creativity, which will blossom your sensual/sexual expression as well.

Right now, many empowered women are deeply entrained in the masculine mode. You are unable to contact and express your deep, passionate desires within yourselves, let alone with your mates. Your softness is covered by the hard shell developed to be as successful as you are. It was/is a survival strategy, necessary to cope in the environment you were born into. Nevertheless, there is the loss of the easy, gentle, receptive energy, replaced by the harsh, stiff, biting one that many of you have developed to survive.

Claire: Women have power now, at least in the Western World, but to get there we've had to get hard and strong. That's not bad, just limiting. How can we presence our unique Feminine Soul-self when we are so super-competent? We're busy juggling so many things: making sure everyone is fed, building a career, driving kids to practice, volunteering for committees, caring for sick family, running errands, and keeping it all going at home. Not to mention alone time, spiritual practice, and self-care. Now we need to be more feminine *and* save the planet, too? Can we take on any more?

Somehow there needs to be a shift. There must be an easier and gentler way. Could it be that and we need to do *less* to embrace and express this Divine Self, and live that into the world? We can be who we are and come from a different place, with less exhaustive efforting and masculinized striving. This unveiling and expressing of Feminine essence sounds almost too easy. And yet, it would be a whole new Earth.

Mary Magdalene: My dear, you are on to something. Good Goddess, you're getting it! For centuries, my story (and all the Marys) has been mis-represented. This is why we come to you and implore that this be set straight. We understand this has been a challenging journey for you, as it defies your expectations and ideas. Yet that does not mean this Truth is to be avoided, dear one. This is a powerful piece during an equally powerful time. It speaks of the church and their direct misalignment with Truth and Love, using power over, rather than power-from-within.

The church fathers have, for centuries, silenced the voice of the feminine, in themselves and others, to devastating consequences, as you see in your news today. Allegations yet again of sexual misconduct and cover-ups at high levels of the Catholic hierarchy are again revealed. While this news is devastating, it is also necessary. What are they to say for themselves in the here and now, when there has been death and destruction in the name of their God for millennia?

What of the Cathars, The Pure Ones, almost a million strong, who practiced The Way in southern France and northern Italy until they were summarily exterminated by the dominant Catholic authority? Will their story ever be told? We cannot understate the devastation of eliminating those who carried the seed of the Christed One (Yeshua) through Magdalene and her legion of followers. This includes her seed-children, as well as those who carried The Way, as was taught by the one you know as Jesus the Nazarene.

Reclaim the Patriarchy

You are compelled to return to the story, your spiritual obsession, time and time again because the Truth must be revealed. Similarly, the message must be conveyed, in practices and teachings of love and light. This is the reclamation of the Feminine Divine and the reunion of the male God with his female

Goddess. This is redemption for all those on the planet who are living (and hurting) in female bodies because of the mistruth of your Godhood that has been perpetuated.

These are harsh words and difficult to stomach, but the time is here for the patriarchy to be revealed and shifted. It is not about killing the father or overthrow of leadership, be it political or religious. It is not even about ending the patriarchy. Rather, begin something fresh that honors and supports a new way of being, that has not yet been tried: partnership and collaboration. When the innovative appears, the out-dated will crumble and fall away. Develop original models and means of relating that are not based on the assumed structures and processes so embedded in your culture that you do not even realize they are there.

Take back the patriarchy. Take it out of yourselves and support this in others, too. It is not about "bad men" out there. It is about recognizing all the ways that we collude and collaborate with injustice, disempowerment, and mistruth.

Your culture is closer than you think to making this shift. Remain open and aware of self-responsibility and leadership, even when it is uncomfortable and unwelcome. Divine the feminine, in yourself and in others. A beautiful and sacred act. Encourage women on this journey to keep honoring and trusting their own wisdom and Truth. Though it may not go as planned or expected by conventional wisdom, that doesn't mean anyone is even slightly off track.

You are all exactly where you need to be: in the arms of the Mother God. She is also you. Love you. As you learn to love her, you love you. This is potent, for it unmakes all the years, centuries, and lifetimes that appear hideous and unlovable. And you all shared that. Whatever side of the sword you were on, it was not in beauty and love. So love that which is calling to be loved. Trust that as you do this, love (which is the Divine) will love you back. You will blossom, into the heart of the Divine She. This is who you really are.

Fierce, Fabulous Force

The feminine is alive. She is juicy, radiant, and whole. She is emerging again, after years, decades, eons undercover. For so long, it has been so unsafe for the dynamic, expressive, and co-creative force of women to be presenced in society. Unfortunately, in many cultures and even in our so-called advanced society, it is still NOT okay for women to express their full passion, power and ingenious spark. These times are ending. It is not a moment too soon.

Mary Magdalene: Yes, dear. As this fierce, fabulous, feminine force becomes focalized into human experience, it is a time of reclaiming. For many, the risks have been great and largely unavoidable, due to issues of safety. These fears and dangers have been very real. They are direct reflections of the lesson each Soul chooses to incarnate around. For many women, it is a time now for remembering and repairing that which was lost, stolen, or damaged.

There have been many who have suffered at the hands and minds of leaders (we are sorry to say, mostly men) who desired control. This is the outcome of greed, which is the out-picturing of deep lack and disconnection. These men, while well-intentioned on a Soul level (remember, we always choose our teachers) certainly inflicted pain and suffering on the physical level. This must end.

So for many women, the school of their greatest learning has been through pain, suffering, and humiliation. It is challenging, but through the infliction of the wound and the recovery therein, great growth occurs for each who travel that path.

As the Divine Feminine awakens, not only does Spirit in Goddess form return, but balance and partnership are re-aligned. For without the Divine Feminine, the Divine Masculine can only be out of kilter. The re-emergence of the Sacred Feminine is a signal that it is time for the Divine Divorce to end. Restore and re-pair the Divine couple to their heavenly throne in your culture's religious theology.

The balance in union of masculine and feminine as a spiritual model is coming back into play. For if humans are made in the image and likeness of God, and there clearly are women (along with females in every life form), where is the Goddess? Where is the She-God we are made in the image and likeness of?

Claire: Certainly if God creates universes, this all-knowing, sacred power would not forget and leave half the population out of the Divine recipe? It makes no sense that we have swallowed this explanation (that women have no Souls) for millennia. Have we been tortured, killed, and raped into submission and acceptance of what is? Women properly empowered and aligned with our own God-like essence—our Goddesshood—certainly would not be allowing these abuses to our bodies and our planet. We would not allow our men to harm our sisters in any manner.

Only when we are disconnected from Source and our innate divinity can this be so. A collective amnesia occurs when too many have forgotten this Truth. We only need look to nature to see the balance and wholeness of other creatures in partnership, male and female, in the co-creation of life. (This is not to be confused with advocating heterosexuality as the only true path.)

We are awakening a new partnership, in divinity and in humanity. All spiritual texts say in various forms, "as above, so below." It is this union of masculine and feminine in partnership that we are striving for.

Ironically, as the Feminine Spirit awakens, she allows the possibility for each of us to contain both feminine and masculine qualities. As we fully awaken the feminine aspect, we contain and express the polarities within each of us. We honor the opposites in each other, and the Divine Masculine arises as well. Coming fully into partnership with our mate (of either gender), there are more options than being male or the pseudo-male of feminism.

Mary Magdalene: Yes, for this has previously been the only choice for successful females to survive and thrive in this world for several thousand years. It is an exciting time, as this awakening of the feminine signals the re-emergence of the Divine Union and sacred marriage, the "Hieros Gamos" of old.

Hieros Gamos *was the ancient rite of anointing and marrying the King to his Goddess/Priestess bride. This sacred ritual was a religious and a political practice, in a time when nature, harvest, land, and Spirit were held differently than in your current religious paradigm. The belief was that when nature (represented by the Priestess as Goddess and bride) was honored, the harvest from which all life depended would be plentiful. This act represented a spiritual partnership with the land, which the King held dominion over politically. This was far different than the subduing and manipulation of nature which we see common in the agricultural practices today.*

There was a long-held awareness that, for life to survive, there had to be balance and union between all parts of the whole. There are no opposites, nothing to be against. When we honor and accept the positive aspects of each, the differences pale in comparison. There is deep play and joy in the union of the Divine partners, and we are fortunate to participate in this awakening.

More than any other material in this book this long message altered my perception about the potential that the awakened Sacred Feminine could have on our society. As I was receiving this Divine Download from Magdalene, I suddenly recognized a huge, yet hidden, disadvantage that was embedded in the feminine psyche. I saw and sensed just how big the impact of this shift in consciousness could be. Owning my feminine divinity has been subtle some ways, and yet radically life altering.

The Practice: Vision Map

Vision Mapping is a powerful process that combines intention setting with the immediacy and simplicity of collage. I call it a Vision Map because it shows you where you are going, and some of the possible stops (and companions) along the way. Create a collage using images and words from magazines that express your dreams, intentions, and/or ideal about some aspect of your life.

This Vision Map focuses on relationship of masculine and feminine in your life (the outer manifestation). Alternately, you could also express your own inner marriage—the balance of feminine and masculine in you—or your Divine Feminine.

You can choose images that reflect where you are, as well as where you want to be going. Include things you want to manifest in your life. Also pick out images (and words) that you are drawn to, even if you don't understand the meaning or message. (You will at some point, trust me.) I am convinced this super-powerful manifestation tool triggers something deep in the psyche that causes these images to show up in physical form. It's like filling out an order form at a sandwich shop. Be careful what you ask for, you just might get it!

1. Start with a large piece of cardboard or poster board.

2. Add the *Consecration* practice (mentioned later, see page 147) to really create dynamic impact in identifying and creating your dreams from a deeper place of Spirit. Pray and set an intention for the focal point of this Vision Map.

3. Collect images and words from magazines that express your ideal relationship, your own inner marriage and/or Divine Feminine self. The images don't have to make sense, just choose ones you are drawn to. They reveal their message later.

4. Create a collage, using glue, tape, or thread to affix your images.

5. Embellish the overlapping images by painting and/or drawing. Add hand lettering for words or phrases that are meaningful.

6. Place your Vision Map somewhere you will see it, even if just in passing as you walk through a room. (It doesn't need front-and-center placement to be effective.) This step is important. Seeing your collage triggers the unconscious in powerful ways.

7. Use this as a reminder for your daily intending and manifesting, then watch it unfold. This is truly magical.

New View on God

The comparison of women to men and the masculine ideal is reflected in the current cultural ideals and stereotypes of God. Even as women are blatantly challenging these societal reflections, remnants are still evident everywhere. In Western Judeo-Christian culture, men relate and form a gender reference to a face of Divinity personified as male. This archetypal connection affirms and empowers a core sense of being and belonging for men, starting at a very young age. No wonder they dominate our culture! The implication, learned early on, is that men are god-like, while to be female is not Divine. Within this belief system, women will always be in a disempowered, subordinate position to men.

Yet scriptures tell us man is made in the image and likeness of God. So what is woman? Woman is Goddess! Our divinity has a different form—we are the feminine face of God. For millennia we were told otherwise. It's time to challenge that belief and change our mindset. The disconnection from our God self is a deep psychic scar to be healed. Embracing this shift in consciousness is staggering to consider.

As aspects of divinity, we are not pawns or playthings of a white-robed, Father God in the sky. Reclaiming our gender-referenced divinity is not esoteric, but inherently pragmatic and timely. Male dominance has put us in grave danger on our planet. We are at a critical moment. For humanity to evolve and thrive, women need to be fully empowered alongside men. We are Goddess, and can offer our gifts and talents in physical form as co-creative experiments in Godhood. We manifest our purpose more fluidly, when know who we really are: expressions of the Divine.

Sacred Mystery © 2014 Claire Sierra

Chapter 5

Embodying Feminine Essence

Beauty Power

As the Divine Feminine awakens in each of us, who we know ourselves to be naturally changes. As our core identity shifts, we hold ourselves differently and move in the world from this new space. We relate to ourselves and our lives from a deeper, wider place. We tap into skills and powers we did not know exist.

One area to be reclaimed is beauty. While beauty can be superficial or artificial, it carries a quality of Soul within it. It is a complicated energy dynamic of its own, a muse that women are taught to admire, court, and worship, starting at a young age. Women are given mixed messages of criticism and encouragement for the cultivation of beauty power. Despite this complexity, we are simply and intrinsically drawn to things, experiences, and people that are beautiful.

For so long, women have been cultivators of beauty, reaching far back into our earliest recorded history. Whether this began as a form of self-care—along with eating and sleeping—or for pleasure, commerce, or social advancement, women have long used practices to enhance their physical form. Such practices can be tools of power and prestige. But regardless of the underlying motive, beauty has been a path that most women have followed, whether for their own enjoyment or for other reasons.

In most cultures, without many options to create personal or professional success, women used beauty to improve social status and to access places of power, often through marriage. This provided more comfort and acquisition of resources, which was perceived as a better life. Ironically, that was not always the case, as powerful men could be cruel and ruthless—in fact, their positions of power might make that more likely. Nonetheless, the strategy prevailed. As a result, the pursuit of beauty has become maligned as superficial. And for some, it is just that.

For many women, then and now, physical beauty is assumed to be a measure of self-esteem and core value. Yet, this external focus often masks insecurity or inner chaos. This "beauty mask" is often, ironically, an expression of low self-worth. Looking good on the outside can conceal vulnerability and the inner disaster that one's life may be. While this can create a good façade, to continue the trajectory of this path generally leads to disappointment and despair when one's glamour fades. As this false self collapses, our Feminine essence yearns for authentic expression.

Soul Essence

Our Soul Essence is the quality that we express when we are just being ourselves. It is not learned, it is who we are: unique and unrefined. This could be joyful, light, hopeful, compassionate, truthful, or clear. It might look classic or organic, polished, frilly, or athletic. No matter what package we put ourselves in, or what we are doing, we are radiating this essence in our own unique package.

Beauty that exudes from our essence has a quality of Soul, which is why we are so compellingly drawn to it, in life and in art. And what are women, if not beautiful? Yet it is not the airbrushed artifice of stereotyped ideals, but in the unique expressions of our diversity that we see true beauty in women. We immediately recognize those who radiate Soul Beauty, often regardless of outer appearance. As we celebrate the rich diversity of size, shape, and color, we all naturally shine, regardless of our adherence to cultural ideals.

In the awakened Divine Feminine, our beauty shines from the inside out. We radiate our beauty when we are fully alive and connected with Feminine Soul, our essence self. Our beauty lies in knowing and *embodying* our uniqueness—really loving ourselves for it. A woman who owns her core sense of self—knowing who she truly is (in all her ordinary magnificence) and why she is here—is a beautiful woman. And size/shape/color/age does not matter. She is radiant from within.

Beauty from Inside Out

Mary Magdalene: This is a major piece that you tapped into today. Your heart has long had a yearning and inspiration with regard to Beauty and Soul that for years was not popular and has not yet been expressed. This connects strongly to the awakening of the Sacred Feminine.

For who are women, if not the cultivators of beauty? You are beauty in form. And the love of beauty has been a trait of women since the inception of time and before, in the non-physical world from which we all come.

Not that the male is unattractive or cannot cultivate beauty. Again, the feminine can be in either male or female form. Men with interest in beauty have a strong inner feminine that they have not lost contact with. Celebrate this.

For women, the focus on outer beauty and beauty power, especially as it has been celebrated in youth, is an aberration of a sacred essence of Feminine Soul. And it results from power imbalance of male over female. Women learned to cull power in areas where it pooled. Beauty power is a potent intoxicant that has yielded great status and reward for many women.

However, this focus on superficial attractiveness is not often without dire consequence. As one's beauty fades, the external focus of power is lost. What is left behind is a hollow, empty, contorted shell. The long-neglected inner life is a vacuum.

The Practice: Be Your Beauty

Sometimes we are known for things that we've been taught or trained to be, that are not even intrinsic to our nature. We are not what we wear, or how we look, but these are expressions of how we feel about ourselves. This effects how we show up in our life, and the world responds accordingly. Often we just step in line with others around us.

I've become aware that every few years, as I change and grow inside, my clothes, shoes, and hair (or my "look") change on the outside (deliberately or unconsciously), sometimes dramatically and sometimes subtly. As I call in new aspects of my Divine purpose, stretching myself personally and professionally, what I am drawn to surround myself with changes.

These everyday things do impact us. You get to choose. You can change your sense of self from the inside out, as well as the outside in. Make a conscious choice, if you want to create a divinely inspired purposeful life. Shine your essence, live from there, and be true to your own beauty. Beware, it can be addicting.

1. Take time daily to connect with your essence, your intrinsic worth as a *being*, rather than your worth for *doing*. Allow yourself to be your true Self, inside and outside.

- What qualities do you innately express? Who are you when all the masks are down?

- See if others around you are uncomfortable at first and try to pull you back into the form, role, or package they are used to. Do they applaud? True allies will support your changes.

2. Notice a difference in how feel when you are more intentional and aligned with what you are surrounding yourself with, whether it's clothes, environment, or people. This could be color, texture, or style, a change of season or interests. This affects how you shine your essence to the world.

3. Look at or think about your wardrobe. Is your closet filled with things you secretly hate but think you are supposed to wear? Journal about:

    - Do your clothes (colors, shapes, textures, styles) and accessories show who you really are?

    - What about your hair, makeup, and jewelry?

    - What else do you notice or are you curious about?

4. Journal about your understanding of your own Essence and worth as a being. Consider these questions:

    - What do you really like about yourself?

    - What do others praise you for?

    - How aligned with your Essence do these compliments feel?

    - Do the compliments reflect who/what you want to be?

    - How would like to be known or seen instead?

Light from Within

Mary Magdalene: There is another aspect to beauty that does not rely solely on the outer manifestation of form. Draw on the light and life from within. The inspiration of beauty for women at any age is a key component to reclaim the Divine in feminine form. Not to focus on the superficial form on the outside. You have the multi-million dollar beauty and fashion industry devoted to this. Rather, to highlight the repression of this ideal in most women.

Many women, if not most, do not see or value their own beauty, other than what they believe is true about their outer form. What women believe about their beauty depends 100% on what the culture at large has taught them about their own value and worth, physically. Women are so socially and externally referenced in this regard that they cannot see their own light and beauty when it is not reflected in the cultural ideal. Fat, tall, skinny, dark, light – each one has a list of where they do or do not "measure up." Yet you each bear beauty beyond measure! In repressing and denying this, you suffer. You reject yourselves as beings of light and power.

When a woman is in full, radiant contact with her beauty, from the inside out, she conveys a light that is magnificent for all to see. To be in the energy vortex of that is to be in a healing presence of light. Women desperately need to connect with this sacred inner beauty, to see how this expresses into form as outer beauty. This is a glorious and delightful experience to behold.

As you stand stronger in your inner light and radiance, others will naturally be drawn to you. Rather than see this as about or from you, they will want to be around you to develop this wisdom quality in themselves. Some will, of course, see it as coming from you and think it is not available for them, so then your work is to show them otherwise. It is not for you to convince them, for the proof will be in their own "beauty pudding," so to speak.

As women see and feel changes in their own ability to love and value themselves as Divine beings of light in female form, this will be conveyed outwardly also. The feedback in 3D form will be tangible and effective as reinforcement. As this occurs, it will validate the process and activities for those who are engaged.

That is all. For now we are complete, though we are quite excited at the breakthrough this dialogue triggered. You are well on your way.

The Practice: Shine Your Light

Cultivate your inner light. This is your radiance, which shines as your true inner beauty. We can use this awareness practice when going through a phase of feeling small and invisible. Address that belief, and also start projecting your essence energy into the world. So when you go out in public, you show up. Your magnetism can be a strength that you use to bring people and opportunities to you. Radiant and alive, you attract people and situations that you have a Divine destiny to meet. As I began using this practice in my life, I noticed that people responded and reacted to me differently. I learned to own and manage my radiance, choosing situations and circumstances wisely. Allow yourself to be visible and shine. It always feels good.

1. Journal about what you feel sense or believe your Essence to be. Hint: This is a core quality you bestow when you walk into a room. You may not know it, but those close to you do. Ask them for clues, as well as in your prayer and meditation practice.

2. Bring your awareness to your inner being, especially at the crown of your head. Remember your essence quality.

3. Say to yourself, "I am _____." Allow this light to drop into your body.

4. Turn up the flame of your inner light. Radiate your Essence. Shine it out from your eyes and heart, as you silently repeat your "I am…" statement. Exude this light from all parts of your body. Feel what happens as you do so.

5. Notice the difference in how you relate to yourself, physically, emotionally and energetically, when you connect in to your Essence light.

6. Notice how you relate to others. Share this with them if you feel inspired. Be aware of other outer reactions or responses, as well.

7. Journal about your experiences with this practice, as it can change over time.

Embody Bliss

Mary Magdalene: We wish to shift into a discussion about how you can begin to bring this Divine Feminine awakening into your world and life more.

It begins with you. Recognize your own innate, intimate relationship with the strong, sweet, silky, slippery essence of your own female body. Not only the sensual part, but include that, too. For far too long, this has been misconstrued and sexualized, demonized and disconnected. Too many women are completely disengaged from your own Feminine Essence, which is Soul. Each of you has this, and it is completely different, as you are each unique individualized expressions of the Divine in human form.

This is to be celebrated, though we understand that for so long the body of the woman was a thing to be despised, used, and discarded. And for some in this lifetime, that is still so. Regardless of where you are on the planet, the experience of living in a woman's body is charged and dangerous at times. Protection and safety are still valid concerns. And when one is afraid, it is not the best experience of embodied aliveness.

When you are able to connect with your essence—the beauty and truth in your body—there is an energy of bliss. It is a form of alignment and congruence that feels charged yet centered, energized yet focused, akin to "controlled chaos." When one experiences this level of heightened electric sensuality, it is at once rapturous and radiant. While easily confused with sexual ecstasy, this is an Eros that is self-referenced and self-contained, disengaged from any co-mingling of mind or body of another. This state is magnetic, and many may be attracted and willing to engage.

As you start to connect with this energy in your body, it feels animated and lively, sometimes even unruly. Therefore, it can be slightly uncomfortable. This is a kind of experience in your body that most usually have privately with a lover, rarely alone, rarer still in a non-sexual encounter in public, like going to the market, library, or post office. To maintain this energy while out in the world is high art. It requires the poise of full containment; this is wild, expressed, Divine Feminine sensual presence.

While it is not sexual, per se, in almost all cultures it has become sexualized and therefore the association remains. To feel this full, wild, bliss state and know this will not be expressed sexually, is rare play for most women. Those who know this experience have often been labeled whore, witch, or crazy. The experience of containing this energy is like enclosing a wild tiger in a glass cage. She is fully visible, transparent, but unable to touch or be touched.

In this place, there is a self-referenced wholeness which implies, "I am an alive, vibrant woman in full power. Look, but don't touch and NO you cannot take any. This is my energy to own, embody, and share at will. I choose when, where, and with whom I express this energy."

Your present culture does not have much space for this embodied immanence. But that is all the more reason for its cultivation. It courts you like a wildcat: pacing, silent and strong, ready to leap. It is this power and presence that your time and land need now, more than ever. And you are coming close.

The Practice: Body Prayer

Take time daily to connect with your essence in its pure aliveness, within your body. Allow yourself 5-10 minutes daily for this practice. (Of course, you can take longer.) This can be added to or rotated with other practices you have already integrated into your daily life. I notice that when I do this, even for just 5 minutes, I feel more connected with myself and more comfortable, open, and relaxed in my body.

1. Breathe deeply into your belly. Let your breath drop below your ribs, down into your hips and legs, so that your breath feels full and slow. Sense yourself as wide and solid, breathing deeply.

2. Connect and ground yourself. Link your breathing to the Earth below you on each inhale and exhale. You might be drawn to stand, sit, or move from the ground.

3. Visualize the bowl of your pelvis filling with breath and energy; feel it fill and empty.

4. Connect with your Soul Essence by recalling your "I am _____." statement. (See "Shine Your Light," page 135.)

5. Let your sensuality and aliveness rise up inside you. You might feel sensations: a tingling or flickering of energy moving. This could feel like joy, heat, pleasure, pressure, or discomfort.

6. Allow your hands to be open, or let any of your fingers to gently touch your thumb. Let your body to start to move.

7. Allow movement to come from whatever part (or parts) of your body that wants to lead. This could be an area that needs gentle stretching or is sore or injured. Maintain the connection you feel with the Earth and with your Self. Let the movement come from this strong, grounded, open connection. This might look like dancing, yoga, stretching, Tai Chi, or any other form of movement you've learned or seen. It may be completely new. It could be gentle, easy, or vigorous.

8. Notice what it feels like to do this at home in a private space. As you feel comfortable, practice doing this in other moments and situations of your life. Try it when you are alone, as well as around others, but only in settings or situations where you feel safe and secure.

Wisdom Reclaimed

Early on in the process of developing this book, Mary Magdalene encouraged me to write about themes that I taught in my work with women. At first, I resisted adding material that was not a direct download from her, but relented with her consistent encouragement.

As I explored Feminine Soul more and more deeply, I recognized how various aspects of my past wove into the mysteries of the Divine Feminine being reclaimed by women today. Sometimes it seemed like entirely different lifetimes from who and where I was now. (Sound familiar?) I recognized threads of my purpose that connected various streams of life experience into wisdom that was starting to converge as this new sacred work.

Honoring Our Cycles

One thread in my work is to increase our awareness of our female fertility cycle and honor our menstrual cycle. So hidden and shamed for most women, it called out to be reclaimed. This, of course, relates directly to the Sacred Feminine and the mysteries of the priestess. For years, I led *Coming of Age* ceremonies for teen girls and *Reclaiming the Menstrual Matrix* workshops for women, about the beauty and wisdom of the female body, with a decidedly non-medical, creative approach.

By exploring a simple, practical, and slightly mystical perspective on our body's innate intelligence, women develop a different relationship to it and our emotions. As women unlock the mystery of their fertility cycle, they learn to listen to their body wisdom, make peace with "that time of the month," eliminate PMS, and embrace menopause.

By shedding the perspective of "the curse" and honoring the power within, our bodies naturally respond differently. As we connect with our own feminine rhythm and pace, we become aware of our personal roller coaster of emotions, often connected to the pattern of our hormonal cycle. This may or may not always be in step with what our ego (our persona) or our life-routine demands. In fact, it may be just the opposite. On busy days when we have physical exercise or outings planned, we may feel a craving for quiet, stillness, and solitude. Our family, workplace, or friends may need us when we want to be alone. Sometimes we may need to be away from the car, phone, and constant electronic messaging. Other days, those activities may suit us just fine.

Our outer focus on success, achievement, or taking care of everyone else's needs may start to fade or increase during certain times. This can often be in step with the phases of the moon. Our work needs become different. We can challenge the importance we give to those external structures or authority. Often, we are taught (even encouraged) to discount "that time of the month." Yet real truths emerge when we no longer are overtaken by our estrogenic urges to "be nice," caring for and nurturing the whole world. Paying attention to those patterns of thought and feeling can be highly illuminating.

Tuning to Our Cycles

At certain times in our monthly cycle we speak more boldly and that can be difficult for others to hear. While we may need to learn how to best deliver the messages that are welling up (or exploding) inside of us, we generally do not need to sublimate and suppress them. That serves no one and only wreaks havoc, ending in frustration, burnout, exhaustion, malaise—even anxiety and depression at times.

This is a journey into an area of female experience that is often overlooked and scorned. Yet from it, we can reap great knowledge, understanding, and wisdom in how we operate as women — mentally, physically, emotionally, and spiritually. These truths are ancient. By tuning into this rhythm, we can better understand our fluctuating desires for intimacy, solitude, socializing, and relationship. Some times of the month are more ripe for connecting than others. Our sensuality changes and with that, interest in sexual contact waxes and wanes. Once we become aware that these biological urges are running us, we can make choices that support our bodies as the blessings they are. When we track and understand the cycle of our fertility, we can choose whether to engage in baby-making or not. This is powerful medicine for our lives. We reclaim this power from the medical establishment and pharmaceutical industry, which often just want to subdue, control, or make the upset, emotional, angry woman go away.

Attuning to our cycle may require us to look at and live our lives differently. Living from a place that is aligned with our own feminine rhythms, we find ourselves more whole and holy. Society, which runs on clock time, may not like that. As women center and cycle with the phases of the moon in our bodies, we connect to life that is fluid and alive. These patterns are deeper, older, and more primal than the city or suburban culture we live within. This is a key as we start a new world that honors and embraces both the masculine and the feminine.

As we tune in to our body wisdom and listen to the truth that emanates from within, we connect into the larger forces around us on the planet. I love knowing this. We cease to feel overwhelmed by the bombardment of images and information designed to distract and disconnect. As we ally with the natural flow of our bodies, we harmonize with the natural world as human members of the greater family of beings that inhabit this lovely planet. This potent reconfiguring of our reality can only bring more wholeness and healing to ourselves, individually and collectively.[2]

The Practice: Cycle Awareness

In this practice, you will learn how to tap in to a vast reservoir of embodied feminine wisdom. You will need a calendar or day planner so you can easily note, chart, and reflect upon what is happening with you. You can also use a journal or notebook, but it's a bit more difficult to track patterns visually.

Most women have 28-32 day cycles, from when they start their menstrual period or "moon flow" to when it starts again, approximately a month later. That is the full cycle that you will start to pay attention to. Some of us are regular like clockwork; others vary by a few days or more. There is no wrong way to cycle, it is your body wisdom.

Doing this over the course of months and years, you can learn so much about physical, mental, and emotional rhythms that are innate to you. Cycle Awareness guides you in learning to track your own inner patterns, which can be immensely valuable in your life in myriad ways. Practically speaking, you can begin to plan your life events around your knowledge of where your energy and mood are likely to be. You can also take corrective action (damage control) with the hindsight of your calendar. As you do this for several months, patterns will start to emerge.

A word to women who are menopausal or beyond cycling: observe, monitor, and record your own moods. See if and how they coincide with the phases of the moon or other "external" forces. You are probably

---

[2] Please note, I am not giving medical advice. Be responsible and empowered in working with your healthcare practitioner. Apply these ideas as is appropriate for your personal body-mind system and use common sense.

still being influenced by hormonal factors and patterns may emerge, though perhaps differently or not to the same degree than when you were cycling.

(Please note, I am not giving medical advice. Nor do I wish to encourage you to be irresponsible in following your healthcare provider's direction. You have wisdom about your health that is wise to hear and heed. This practice adds to your knowledge of your body. Sharing your observations with your practitioner is common sense; use it as you see fit.)

1. Mark your calendar or day planner the first day you begin your monthly moon blood flow or menstrual "period." That becomes "Day 1" of your cycle, which ends when you start bleeding again. Start to notice what is "normal" for you, without judgment or comparison. If you know how long your cycle is, write those numbers in the corner of your calendar, from 1-30, or whatever. (Most women fall within a 28-32 day cycle.) Or do this daily or weekly, counting as you go.

2. To track your hormonal rhythm, start by noticing your moods and thoughts and how they may cycle throughout your day and week. (Eventually, you will look at the whole month.) Make short notations, using a word, phrase, or symbol. This will enable you to track patterns and preempt suffering.

3. Explore and research the biology of the hormonal cycle and how that works, if that interests you.

4. Make note of physical issues as they arise, especially chronic patterns. They can be connected.

5. Add notes about life events and activities. Since you're working with your calendar, that's probably already happening, so you are simply syncing up your awareness between inner and outer events.

6. Pay attention. You are the expert and authority here. It's your body, your experience. For too long, we have been taught to submit to the authority of others, disregarding our own inner terrain.

- Do you seek quiet after busy weekends?
- Do you crave specific kinds of activities or company at certain times and not others?
- Are some emotions more volatile and nearer the surface at particular times of your month?
- Are there consistent thoughts and patterns of speaking coming from your mouth at a predictable time?

Sacred Feminine Creativity

As this writing meditation process about Feminine Soul deepened and opened, I began to muse about creativity as a sacred act: the spiritual essence of the creative process itself. I've long felt that all creation is Divine art, coming from Source to and through me into the world. It's a shamanic process of mediating between the worlds of Spirit and matter (here on earth.) All we need to do is look around in wonder. In ideal situations, when I am deeply engaged in the creative process, it feels sacred and holy to me. My favorite moments in art-making are when time falls away and I am in the flow of this Oneness. I love it when a creative act feels like a holy moment: time stands still, the heavens open, and the Divine is present and pours herself forth through me. This is so rich and juicy.

I realized that there was a new place where the two concepts of creativity and consecration meet. This led me to a new verb—"consecreation"—combining *consecrate* and *create*. *Consecration*, according the Merriam-Webster dictionary, means to dedicate to a sacred purpose, it is a ceremonial act, honoring something or someone in a manner that is sanctified and holy. *Create* means to produce or bring into existence. *Consecreation*, therefore, is creating acts of beauty in an open, holy relationship with the Divine; to ceremonially intend the creation process to be a sacred experience.

Our creative energy comes from Divine, so what happens when we acknowledge and honor it? *Consecreation* is the act or intention of allowing the creative process to be sacred and infused with Spirit. We can't force that inspiration happen, but we can invite, intend, and invoke it in any moment when we start to create something. Infusing our creative acts with Spirit is pure, untapped potential. When I do this, I am always delighted by juicy goodness that results.

As these thoughts developed, I brought them to Magdalene, to see what her input might be. As always, she had much to share.

Mary Magdalene: Today we wish to discuss this aspect of the Divine co-creative union more. While it is often true that the Feminine is the receptive force, she is also generative and creative. The masculine is expressive and productive, but in a manner and style that is wholly different. This is the model that your culture is accustomed to. You are so accustomed to this outer-focused, dynamic, creative force that you assume is the only direction toward growth.

While growth is good, we need only look to nature and her cycles to recognize (re-cognize: to think again, to have renewed thought) that life is not balanced if it is only and always growing. Observe the cycle of life all around you. There is no growth without return, retreat, and decay. These are necessary parts to the cycle, and yet have become demonized in a culture that only values the outward, product-oriented, results-driven creative process. "Go, go, go, more is better," seems to dominate and seep from the social consciousness of your times.

Yet there is another kind of creativity—reflective, intuitive, organic, and generative. It is life-giving and nurturing, characterized as feminine in form. We are urging the increased expression of this creativity in you and those coming to you. This is not the masculinized version, where you get an idea, follow steps and make a "thing." While that process is good for certain outcomes, it is not the whole of creativity.

Intuitive Expression

Instead, the creative feminine pattern is more liminal and intuitive. The process is valued more than the product. Though the completion of a product is achieved, at the outset it is not the sole focus or conceived as an endpoint. The initiate must make time and space for such expression. She (or he) must first create the time and space around her. Clear away distractions and interruptions, as well as you are able.

Next enter a reflective, meditative mode. From here, pose a question or curiosity such as, "What does my heart wish to create today?" or "I wonder what form, color, shape or texture wants to emerge and express through me right now?" Engage the practice by opening and surrendering to a deeper form of listening. This is not always easy in a culture that values outcome, productivity, and output so highly.

At first glance, this method may not appear to be highly efficient or fruitful, but it is. There will be immense results when approached in this manner, though paradoxically this cannot be the underlying intent or undercurrent. In fact, in this mode you must set aside standard motivation or ambition, surrendering product/outcome to process. This practice is for the sake of creative self-exploration and Soul expression.

Claire: Wow, thank you. This is amazing, upleveling my awareness about creativity, with an entirely new vision.

The Practice: Sacred Creativity of *Consecreation*[3]

1. Tend your creative space, your Artist Temple. Take time to create a sacred place where your creative exploration will occur. This is your gift to you. It is not necessary to have a big space, just someplace where you feel comfortable—even if it is a card table in the corner of an already-crowded room. (Be sure it's not your dining table that you have to clear and eat at every night, if you can at all avoid that. That's a creativity killer.) Notice whether creating this space feels difficult. Women sometimes have difficulty giving to ourselves, receiving from others (or the Divine), or taking up room. You may have judgments about your creative abilities and self-worth. Let that all go for now.

2. If you are creating through drawing, painting, or collage, lay out paper or canvas and other art materials you plan to use. Use a drop cloth (or an old sheet) if you need to protect the floor or carpet.

3. *Consecreate* the moment by starting with your intention. What do you intend this time to be about? What are you hoping to receive? Some possibilities (there are hundreds) are self-expression, relaxation, self-care, emotional release, or journeying. Use prayer, invocation, offering, intention, and whatever other ritual forms you enjoy. You may want to light candles or burn incense, lavender, or sage. Play inspiring music that suits your mood.

4. Establish a connection to your Divine guides and guardians. Pray to Source (Goddess, God, your preference), asking that the Divine join you and express in and through you.

---

3   *Consecreate* - a new verb combining *consecrate* and *create*. To *consecrate* the process of *creation*; to create in open relationship with the Divine; to make the creation process holy with ceremony and/or intention.

5. Invite in your muse, whoever she might be today. Allow your muse to appear and (if it feels comfortable) flow into you. Let yourself receive any images or messages.

6. You may have received an image of what you wish to create, but it is fine if you do not. It can be best to just let your creation emerge from within you and your muse. Allow the first expression to come to you. Start by simply choosing a color and marking with a line, symbol, texture, and/or shape that you feel drawn to. Using pastels, paint, or whatever materials you enjoy or have handy. Or tear and glue down an image from a magazine. You don't need to have a plan, it will emerge. Just start.

7. Next, see what is coming forth: what next color, line, shape, or image is inspiring you, urging to be expressed? Make that move. Let that flow. If you don't feel it, make it up. Play, have fun, be loose. Don't think too much. Certainly don't stop yet.

8. After several moments, another thought, image, or idea—a color, shape, line, or object—will emerge and be present. Follow the urge. Sometimes you need to wait, be patient. Step back and look. Listen and let that next inspired action come through. You may start to feel a certain energy or rhythm pouring in and flowing through you. Allow that.

9. Surrender. Let yourself deeply hear what is emerging from within, and let this expression come into being. Breathe and release any difficult feelings, thoughts, images, or sensations that may arise with this process. As woman, you are a creatrix. This is your natural state. Allow your muse to reveal herself through you; this is the Divine awakening in you, as you.

10. If your interests are inclined toward movement, music, or poetry, the approach is similar. Harmony, shape, texture, line, tone, and rhythm all have their form. Start with one and let yourself follow this until it is complete. Then allow the next. Continue with the

third, and then onward, until you are fully engrossed in rhythm, lyric, word, or song. Allow this expression to come into being, it is alive in you. Let it come through.

11. You don't have to make "a painting," "a poem," or "a dance." The finished product is not the point, though it is likely that you will end up with something. The result will probably be different than your ego mind would anticipate creating. You might like what you create, you might not. If you don't like it, let it go and try again. Just let it be what it is, and enjoy the unfolding. That's where the joy is.

Temple Home Project

As I dove more deeply into beauty and creativity as reclaimed power centers for women, I wondered how this could be cultivated in our lives. Then I had a dream in which I was engaged in a business project with my husband to make home space sacred. As I awoke, I mused on the images and ideas for a few moments. I saw so much potential for what the dream showed me. I spent several moments scribbling furiously to catch as much as I could before the memory faded, as I knew it would.

Excited by this half-dream, half-conscious vision, I got inspired about creating sacred space in the home. I visualized a complete process for guiding women to make our home environments more sanctified and special, as a way to co-create (or *consecreate*) a life of one's choosing. I saw plans for offering consulting services, with marketing, planning, and messaging ideas to develop this into a full practice. I was totally excited *and* overwhelmed — especially in light of being in the middle of writing this book and carrying it to the world. After that huge dose of inspiration, I knew I needed to have a chat with Magdalene about the meaning and direction of this inspired idea.

Claire: Sorry I am late, it took all day to get here.

Mary Magdalene: Never is it a time for apologies. We just start, here, now. We are pleased with the events that are unfolding. First, we see that you embrace the practices. You catch yourself when you are falling into negative pictures and quite often bask in the loveliness. We are delighted and wish for you to continue. This is the first step. You also sense the sacredness of Beauty, not as superficial but at Spiritual Art.

One primary area of beauty cultivation is in the home. We are delighted with the Temple Home Project *idea that you caught earlier this morning. This has many great applications and we think you can start by writing about this tonight. We will dictate, and you can use later as you wish.*

The "Temple Home" is a concept to awaken people to the idea of home as sacred space. You understand the value of living and being in a space that feels holy, serene, and beautiful. There are several aspects to this, including harmony, design, flow, organization and usability (utilitarian esthetics), and sacred corners (or altars).

Tonight we will give you an overview, some of which you already captured during your meditation this morning when you received the idea. The primary question to answer is what does this have to do with the Magdalene Path and the Mari priestesses? Well, everything.

For one, as Priestesses (and all women of the Divine Feminine are priestesses), temple is our home. And for you, living a secular life with work, children, husband, or partner, home is your temple. Many of you are interested in creating sacred space in work and life as a practice of presence and expression of purpose. The easiest way to create this is in the physical place where you reside the most. For daily expression of joy, create a joyful, lively atmosphere. For a calm, serene experience in life, create a home or office space that exudes this quality.

What we notice is that many are trying very hard to create better lives for themselves, and they are not getting there — not as quickly as they'd like, anyway. Some of this has to do with the environments they occupy.

Rather than look to ancient indigenous or oriental philosophies, which may not relate to your everyday cultural reality, look to the traditions that inspire and enlighten you already. Start by noticing your faith path. Is it primarily contemplative (prayer and meditation), service-oriented, Eastern or Western? Is it practice-oriented, embodied, or creative, traditional or eclectic? How do you connect to Spirit in your everyday life?

Now look at your home. Does it reflect that same quality or character? Begin to determine the values that are driving your everyday affairs. For some, it is family, while for others it may be privacy, social interaction, technology, efficiency, or creativity.

Many people start to notice that they have no idea what their core values are, from a conscious perspective. These are primary motivators, whether you know them or not. Once you begin to identify core values and habit patterns, you can look at your home and see if they are reflected there, or not.

You can amend the disparity between what you aspire to in life and what you actually inhabit at home or workplace. The environmental container is your mold. You can't make a Bundt cake in a brownie pan! This is a major place of manifestation and embodiment.

For many women, the path of joy and the path of beauty are entwined. You and many others like you out there come from a long line of priestesses. Some have families, and some do not. You are the ones who wish for your home place to be sacred, a sanctuary for heart, Soul, and Spirit.

You need a place for your weary Soul to unwind after a day of challenges. (And what day is without challenges?) You can create that space, easily and inexpensively, using items you already own or have always been drawn to. You can identify your Temple Home style using an assessment tool. Then others can use this to start to create that space.

Creating a Temple Home is a process and a practice. It is a joy and a responsibility. It is never-ending, yet always complete. Women have long been kept from the centers of power and privilege, except those we were born or married into. Rarely have women had economic and social status unto themselves that is not begotten through a man. It has been this way for centuries. Though we see this starting to change, and we celebrate this, it is this reason why we create the Temple Home. It is, we dare say, a radical and subversive act of power to claim your space and create an environment of your choosing.

The cathedrals, temples, mosques, and lodges of worship are often places where women are not welcome, at least not fully. We may visit, but rarely have we been in any kind of leadership position. So, for millennia, women have created a separate culture and spiritual practice. We have kept this to ourselves, passed from grandmother to mother to step-daughter, aunt to niece and sister-friend to sister-friend.

Without intending it, women have created a separate spiritual subculture. Hidden for generations, it is becoming unveiled. Now it is time to acknowledge your home as your temple. It is where women have secretly served and worshipped in all forms for centuries.

Regardless of who or what you worship, home is the place where your Soul has its primary expression. Look at the preponderance of home décor shops, gourmet kitchen shops, big-box and discount retailers, and we see how important home items are. There is now even a "depot" for all things home. We see a plethora of magazines, reality, and how-to TV shows, of all manner and design. Home is where the heart is, and your hearts are big and full of surprises.

I was relieved and excited by this Divine Download. I felt calm and guided, though not entirely sure how to proceed. I knew I needed to create a practice that supported these concepts, and from there I would see what would happen. I sensed it would uplevel my own environment, and I trusted that as I did that, the rest would become clear.

The Practice: Create Your Temple Home

To develop your own Temple Home, start with this simple assessment tool.

1. Identify your Core Values. Develop a list of basic ideals from personal preferences and attributes. List the 3-5 tenets that you live and orient your life by. You may have more, but it's likely that you have a few that you truly center around.

   To do this, ask, "What core issues are non-negotiable in my life?" These might be as simple as joy, creativity, freedom, and love, or more esoteric, like elegance, spirituality, or integrity. Whatever they are, they are unique to you. Orient your life around them.

   Below are some ideas to get you going. These values may or may not reflect your ideals, but feel free to start here and create your own list based on your personal standards.

   Values (by no means a complete list!):

Harmony	Partnership
Serenity	Sociability/Entertaining
Love/Connection	Sustainability
Family	Nature/Organic
Tradition	Privacy

Culture/Ethnic heritage	Regeneration/Renewal
Order	Truth
Cleanliness	Simplicity
Control	Elegance
Joy	Hominess/Coziness
Energy/Liveliness	Safety/Protection
Beauty	Progressive
Nurturance	Modern/High Tech

2. Once you've developed your list, *consecrate* the time and intention you have for this project. Use the *consecreation* process (mentioned earlier on page 147) to engage in this as a sacred act. Acknowledge that this is a soulful and holy process that can be filled with joy.

3. Allow the holy desire for sacred space in your home to fill your heart. Visualize your ultimate sacred space. See, feel, sense, and imagine how that can be interpreted into your home. Have fun exploring and creating.

4. Begin creating your Temple Home by interpreting these values, attributes, and visualizations into your physical environment. How would your physical location be different when looked at through the lens of the values, visions, and ideals you hold most dear?

5. Start in one room, or even the corner of a room. Ideally, what would that look like? Are there changes that need to be made, upgrades or deletions?

6. Next, notice which of your listed values are reflected in your living environment?

- Which are conspicuously absent, and why?

- Would you like to be living more of this? How would it be represented?

- What reason(s) do you tell yourself for not creating your space to your desire?

- If money were no obstacle, what would you do differently?

- Using the resources you have, are there changes you could make?

7. Clear your canvas. Go through one room and remove anything that does not hold energy or meaning for you. It may mean removing a pillow you've never liked that was a gift from someone or was a rash purchase in a moment of weakness. Or it could be repainting over a color you never liked but were talked into by a friend or it looked good in a magazine.

8. Develop your palette. Look at what remains, all the things you love. Notice if it feels too cluttered. Remove as much emotional noise from the space as you can. Put all those items to one side. These things create a palette for you to choose from, to use later.

9. Once the room is cleared, go through and clean. It's best if you can partner with a friend. Buddy up and help each other out. If you can, hire someone to do it! Like many things, it is far easier to do with support and teamwork. Remember that you are trying to get to a blank canvas.

10. Once the room or area is physically cleansed, clear the space energetically. Use simple ritual: light candles and burn incense, lavender, sage, or cedar smudge stick. Pray, play music, chant mantra, use sacred symbols or crystals to bring purity and clarity. Do what feels comfortable and is part of your faith tradition. If this is new to you, let yourself experiment.

11. Now decide on the use of this room or area, if you have not already. Feel into the space. With a blank canvas before you and a full palette to the side, you may see possibilities and uses that you had not originally imagined. Allow the holy desire of your Temple Home to fill your heart. Let it tell you how it wants to be expressed.

12. Use your Core Values List (developed above) to remind yourself of the qualities and attributes you intend to imbue into this space. You may want to post the list or even stencil or paint them on a wall to remind you. This is *your* Temple—*you* get to decide.

13. Look at the furniture and its placement. Pay attention to windows, doors, passageways, and light. Move things around to try out how it looks and feels. Doing this with a friend—a Temple Home Cohort—can be tremendously helpful, especially if there are any heavy objects that need to be moved.

    - Do the furniture and objects enhance or detract from the values you intend?

    - If you intend serenity, for example, does a red couch really fit in?

    - If you desire a more spiritual focus, is this the best place for the TV, recliner, and pool table? Do you have artwork or sacred objects you wish to use as reminders?

14. Next, choose an area for creating Sacred Corners. Use a shelf, counter, tabletop, or corner to develop an altar of some type. This need not be a traditional religious or even spiritual altar. It is a place where what you value the most is acknowledged and honored.

    - Use linens, cloth, or beautiful papers to outline and define the space. Napkins, placemats, vintage pillowcases, or table runners work nicely.

- Review the previously removed items, bringing things together in new and unusual ways. Something bland and uninteresting in one room can be repurposed into another and create a whole different effect. Look around your house and use what you have.

- Thinking of this as play and non-permanent is helpful.

15. Finally, *Consecreate* your sacred space. And celebrate! Play music, light candles, burn incense. Take as much time as you like, making offerings, prayers, intentions, and meditation there. You may wish to do this daily as part of your emerging or regular spiritual practice. Many women find this daily touchstone to be a grounding and centering way to orient their life and purpose. Come to your Temple Home as often as you wish. Revise or update it seasonally, or whenever Spirit moves you.

ABCs for Reclaiming Feminine Essence

Mary Magdalene: Today we would like to review the steps to engaging with the Divine Feminine as we see this occurring.

1. **Acknowledge.** *Know that, since the world is sacred in all her parts and pieces, then women and the feminine form are sacred, too — regardless of what women have been told, felt, or experienced. This is the first step in awakening, for unless the lack of the feminine is perceived, it will be impossible to reclaim and remember.*

2. **Believe.** *Develop an awareness that this knowledge of awakening the Feminine Soul is important for humankind if you are to move forward as a species. Only with this belief can you act on the awareness and move forward yourself.*

3. **Create.** Know that the Divine Feminine comes alive in the creative process. Not the creation of product, but the process of opening to the creative force and allowing it/Her to flow. Acknowledging creativity is part of the path at this phase of opening.

4. **Divine Discernment.** Let inspiration lead. The embodiment of Truth flowing to and through you is worth acting on. Act as if this matters. Learn to trust as you organize your life around this guidance. Take inspired action.

5. **Embody.** Consciously engage these teachings in a direct, embodied manner. Take them to heart. Bring the Divine She into your heart and body and see who is there. It is different for each of you, and all paths are sacred. She is alive and willing to come forth, but cannot do so unless invited. Awareness of your ability to be her as a creative, divine being is a crucial piece in this recovery by humanity.

6. **Flow.** Allow yourself freedom to move and create according to your intuition and guidance from Source. This is a key feminine trait and essential strategy in the awakening process of Feminine Soul. It is enhanced with practice and suffocated by neglect.

7. **Gratitude.** Appreciation is the key to beauty, truth, love, and joy. Bliss occurs when we are grateful for all we have and All That Is. It is impossible to feel grateful and unhappy at the same time. Lift yourself up.

8. **HOPE: Heaven on Planet Earth.** Act as if there is glory all around you, for there is! The more you notice, the more there will be. Like attracts like, so "where your attention goes, energy flows."

9. **Invite.** Allow the Divine to flow into and through you, in whatever manner you and She choose. Create time and develop practices that allow you connection with whatever you know as Holy. You are sacred. Trust your Soul.

10. ***Join.*** *Find your sister-friends to celebrate the joys and support the challenges. You are not meant to do this alone. Enjoy the company of your sisterhood.*

We could go on alphabetically in this manner, but we think you get the idea. This is all for today. Work with these. We are complete.

Freedom © 2014 Claire Sierra

Chapter 6

Lessons for Living Larger

Simple, But Not Easy

I was having breakthroughs: engaging, writing, and sorting this project as guided and directed. At times it really flowed beautifully. The process seemed to be slow and long, but I was moving forward nonetheless. Yes! I found the tools and perspective shifts that Magdalene was sharing to be amazingly simple, and yet powerful. I gathered the remaining skills and processes here as Magdalene suggested.

Mary Magdalene: We see you are committed and engaged in this process here, as well as introducing the practices we suggest into your life. Excellent. You no doubt notice that there is information coming from various sources, though it all comes from One Source. Your careful and sharp integration of what you hear from others is wise and fully acceptable, for that is us speaking to you, too.

We notice that, as you create and fulfill your promises, your faith and inner fire build. These practices are part of that development. The platform of your own felt experience, charged by your will and intention, is ever stronger.

The practices we offer are basic but profound. While simple at first glance, they are not easy, for it is in the doing *that the value and the outcome are experienced. And, like many things, the simplest practices are the most impactful because they are most easily integrated into life. So, as this occurs, life becomes magic and sacred every day. And what is NOT amazing about that? Basic everyday life is becoming filled with myth and magic—is that not what you/we are all hungry for?*

We recognize the pressures on your time and accountability. We see the improvement and the deep value that this project brings to you and are pleased. This internal pressure is "by design," meaning you are compelled toward this project, which will ensure that this message is delivered "to those with ears to hear."

It felt good to have the feedback and acknowledgment that what I was implementing was accurate and that the practices I was integrating into my life were having effect. I surely felt the benefits. I was seeing and sensing more potential and possibility, not just for myself, but for others I was working with who took up this path. I knew that my life was going to unfold as a result of this process, in ways I could not entirely see. This naturally led me to think more about what I was intending, creating and visioning. What were my deeper dreams and desires that this project was a reflection of? I sensed that the more consciousness and clarity I could bring, the more imaginative creativity I could allow, would only mean a more magical outcome.

The Practice: Rev-Up Your Holy Desire

"But what does my heart long for?" This is a question I hear from women often. I've felt that confusion, too. A simple question, it should be easy to answer. But *should* is never an empowered direction to follow. "Should" almost always aligns me with other people's goals and dreams, taking me far, far away from my own. It's hard to hear myself if I am tuned into someone else. No wonder there's confusion about our desire.

So often, we are taught not to want what we want. As women, we care for others and often put their needs first. Messages in the media teach us to want, but our culture teaches us to deny those wants. No wonder we lose touch with what our own true yearnings are! Our deepest desires come through our Soul's calling. When we attend to them, they point like arrows on an inner compass to our destiny path, our own True North. Now, let's discover your Holy Desire.

1. How do you want your life to be?

    - If you were reviewing your life, what would you want it to have been filled with? Review this list frequently, nightly is best.

    - What feelings, sensations, and experiences do you want to have?

    - If money or time were no object, what would you want to be doing? Where would you want to be? With whom? Let this bubble up unbidden, without force.

    - Notice if there are any dreams, intentions, or goals you consistently fall short on. Are you being unrealistic, or is there a way you can bring more of that experience into your life?

    - Are they really your desires, or do they belong to someone else?

2. Feel how you will feel when you get that, or achieve that intended outcome. Really allow the good feeling, as you connect with the desire.

3. Rev that up, so that you are in that state for several minutes. Feel the good feelings, the joy and excitement of achieving this desire. Focus more on the emotion, rather than the specific item or experience.

4. A friendly reminder: For best results, it is helpful to include the request, "This or something better, for the best and highest of all Creation." That, or a similar prayer, gives your intention up to the higher wisdom of Source, so that you are not putting upper limits on the creativity of the universe and the blessings that may come your way. Feel free to adapt and use your own words.

Energy Follows Intention

As the full Harvest Moon began to wane, I noticed a shift of my awareness from the outer to the inner. My thoughts were drawn to my goals and intentions: "Where am I going? What is my focus?"

Often, too much of life is lived on auto-pilot. We dash from one task to the next, collapsing in exhaustion at the end of the day, and start again the next. While we might have bigger goals, they tend to be abstract and distant. They seem "out there," and we don't often take the time to bridge the gap from a daily trudge to mindful living. On the Divine Feminine path, creating achievable goals starts with intention—not planning or action. And it is this underlying "come from" that often gets missed.

In the world of manifesting our "dream lives" from the Feminine Soul perspective, intentions are the under-structure of the whole process. They are the unseen force, the inner engine that gets the goal to completion, in abundance, ease, and grace. (Though taking action that backs your intention and "voting with your feet" is important, too.) Your intention is the vision and feeling-place inside you where your action (and goal) comes from. What are you dreaming of? What is the highest, grandest, most creative expression of you that wants to manifest in a particular situation?

In the masculine worldview, we often we focus on a goal and we skip intention. We start at the end and "reverse engineer," creating steps to where we want to go. We can forget to check in with our hearts, bodies, and deeper knowing which is the center of the Divine Feminine.

Energy (and outcome) follows intention. What we think about and focus on tends to gather energy, which creates momentum. This often becomes tangible physical reality: manifestation. We tend to make real what we think about and believe will come to pass. We create a self-fulfilling prophecy.

So if we keep ignoring or downsizing our hopes and dreams, guess what happens to them? Nothing, they go nowhere. Habits, lazy-mindedness, unconscious awareness, and other cultural conditioning seem to figure prominently in this picture. We default to a general black and white worldview, forgetting who we really are as creators of our lives and how grand our options really can be.

We can cultivate a different awareness. When we take time to do this, our days tend to be easy, joyful, and effortless. Synchronicity becomes commonplace and intuitive hits are stronger. Direct downloads from Spirit are clearer when we remember our intention and connection. The quality of interactions are lovely and problems get solved efficiently—unlike "normal," non-intentional, unconscious moments, which can be fraught with challenges and stress.

As I reflected on this, I asked Magdalene to offer her perspective, and this is what she said:

Remember, Believe, Receive

Mary Magdalene: Today we wish to share with you about intention and how it's related to holding, owning, and claiming your power.

When you have an intention in life, large or small, it is like you send a ray of light to something and connect it to you. You create a signal, a beam of light between you and that thing. So, regardless of your intention—to have a beautiful home, to know your Soul's purpose, to have a harmonious relationship, or to find a great dress to wear to a party—the process is the same. It is sometimes easier to practice with smaller physical items, because the results are more tangible and visible than states of being. But the process is the same.

This is a simple process. The challenge comes in 3 aspects: Remember, Believe, Receive. Remember *to do this,* believe *it is possible, and you are worthy to* receive *the fruits of your blessings. Your* remembering *is strengthened when you are more frequently proactive in doing this practice. Then comes a critical pivot point:* Believing *it is possible. Anything is possible, yet you must believe you are capable and worthy of receiving. Know that you are. You are an essence of God, a spark of the Divine.*

Cast aside all previous trainings in lack and loss, knowing that they were correct and appropriate experiences for that time and place of service. They have served you well. You may notice and understand this in others. Now it is time for that training to be complete.

Know how this works and how it feels, along with the impact it has on you and your ability to co-create in your life. Once you truly feel and know that you are worthy of creating your dreams, you will easily begin to manifest them on the material plane.

This is easy to see in basic aspects of your life. You feel hunger. You have an expectation of receiving nourishment in the form of lunch. You know you are worthy, without giving it any thought. All kinds of options from simple to grand are available and appear. There are those in other places who do not have that expectation or sense of worthiness, and as a result they are unable to manifest this for themselves. This is not intended as a judgment, but a statement of fact. It is based on their life experience and what they have been taught to expect for themselves. This can happen in your wealthy nations and in impoverished ones, too.

Intention is the key to manifesting; self-worth and expectation are the pivot points. Notice this, without judgment, when you are not creating something that you want. Your expectation charges your experience. There are deep and subtle levels that are obscured from the light of conscious awareness in your own mind. This touches into beliefs, and there are practices that can help clear unconscious and conscious limiting beliefs, but for now we are complete.

The Practice: Roll Out the Red Carpet

Here's a hidden secret to making a life of your creation. This brief intention setting practice can create great changes in your life experience. Take time to think about your day and how you'd like it to go. As you do this, you external world starts to line up with your inner vision and becomes your life. Creating a joyful, positive future appears to be as simple as creating a happy thought picture about your day. It's an amazing life-management tool—simple, just not always easy to remember to do.

1. Write down your 1-3 main intentions for your life for this year, month, or week. Post them where you will see them, to remind you of your intention. (To supercharge your intended vision and creation, create a Life Vision Map, see page 125.)

2. Spend 3-5 minutes in the morning previewing your day. Do this mindfully, as part of your morning meditation practice, if you have one. Or add it to your morning ritual of brushing your teeth.

3. Allow your attention to rest on the day that is ahead of you. Become aware of how you would like it to go, play by play from start to finish, like you are previewing a movie of your life. Visualize it as clearly as you are able. Use your senses of inner sight, smell, taste, touch, and sound, so that your inner movie exists in a very real form in your mind. Project into the feelings you would like to be having, so they feel real. You might think about:

   - How do you want your daily path to unfold?
   - How do you want to feel?
   - What are your planned activities?
   - How do you want the activities to go?
   - What do you want to experience?
   - Who will you be working/playing with?
   - How would you like those interactions to feel?

4. At the end of the day, as part of your daily winding-down activities, take time to review and journal. Notice and feel gratitude for how easily and effortlessly things worked out for you. Avoid self-criticism or negativity (if it comes up) if challenges arose. Give thanks and move on to another day of feeling good.

Doing From Being

Mary Magdalene: Enjoy your blessings. Relax and allow yourself to really have and enjoy the life you have created for yourself. Right here, right now. Not in some future-perfect version, "When and if…" Instead, let yourself have and regale in the perfection of All That Is. Breathe deep and let all the lists (actions, wants, needs, and desires) go.

Detach from that place inside you that thinks you don't have everything you need exactly as you create and desire it. The "I'd like more of this or better that" keeps you from the eternal present. Now is eternal, because when you actually allow yourself to be there, you will find it is vast and endless. It stretches into eternity, foreverness.

The ego-mind is afraid to hang out there. It fears that if you do not keep up with the endless internal/external lists, you will forget and get lost in eternity. This, we are pleased to report, is actually not possible.

The ego fears that you will lose touch with its incessant driving desires, and that without the pushing self, you will vanish. Nothing could be farther from the truth. In fact, your Soul self starts to show up and shine out. You become in alignment with your actual inner light and Being. Instead of forgetting, there is true remembering. And from that place, life flows and those list-oriented activities actually get done more easily with less effort. More external solutions and interventions show up. You do not have to do it all yourself, yet so much in your culture conspires to tell you the opposite.

You are a nation of codependent entities, counterbalanced by irresolute iconoclastic individuals. Loners or groupers, are both (paradoxically) over-dependent on others, either to keep them separate (alone and afraid, but safe) or are so intertwined with overdoing for others that nothing else (especially from the non-physical world) can step in.

Instead, free yourself from these entanglements. Allow your being *to lead. Let doing arise from this state of being. Inspiration will come, actions will arise. The ego-mind may fight at first, but this is well worth working through.*

Laser of Manifestation

The physical desires that one has can only arrive when there is mastery of the moment. This moment is guided, directed, highly influenced, and sought out by those who can generate a vibrational field that is a request on one hand, and an expectation (with gratitude) of absolute fulfillment on the other. One needs to have confidence and expectancy—asking and receiving in perfect harmony, while being grounded in the vast presence of the blessedness of Now.

This state of grace is for all to experience. Many, if not most do, at one time or another. Now is a time when you can begin to cultivate this presence and state of grace. Simply breathe, relax, request, and allow. *Do this within the context and container of* gratitude *for what is already so blessed, and for what will undoubtedly occur. Within gratitude, there is an absolute expectation of fulfillment. And that attitude needs to be practiced.*

Look for evidence of wealth, and you see wealth. Poverty shines light on more poverty. It is all where you choose to put your attention. Your attention is a powerful laser of manifestation. What you see will indeed grow. Lack will grow, too. It is all about where you place your perspective. Indeed, your focus is powerful. Add spoken or written words to your internal creation process, and the effect is increased a thousandfold. Notice the difference between what you silently think, believe, or want versus what occurs once you speak those things out loud. They either shrivel under the light of conscious reflection and presence, or they manifest and grow exponentially. Look at the power of news, either commercial or hometown gossip. Whatever you focus on grows.

The Practice: Gratitude Journal

If you develop only one practice, make it this one. The cultivation of gratitude can radically alter your life. Gratitude increases awareness and expands presence in the moment. It is impossible to feel unhappy and grateful at the same time. Each morning as you arise, or in the evening as you settle down to sleep, take time to count your blessings.

1. Breathe deeply. Let all the actions, wants, and desires go. Disconnect from all thoughts of lack and need, bringing your attention fully into the present, now.

2. Make a list or jot into a journal, noting 10 things daily that you feel grateful for. These may be as mundane as your favorite cozy slippers warming your feet, sunshine outside, a warm place to sleep, your loving cat purring on your lap, or the ability to choose what you have for dinner tonight. What gifts we are surrounded by, yet blind to!

3. Allow yourself to feel gratitude for your life. Appreciate yourself and all your efforts to make your life and your world a better place. Breathe deeply.

4. If at first you can't *feel* your gratefulness, as least *think* about your blessings and gifts. Make your list. Dig deep, really take in all the good you are surrounded by. The feelings will follow.

5. Detach from the place inside you that thinks you don't have everything you need exactly as you create and desire it. This is an illusion, a by-product of a culture of disconnection and lack. It appears very convincing and results in *FEAR*. (*False Evidence Appearing Real*)

Planetary Wave

Mary Magdalene: We are delighted to have these moments to share this with you. We feel your shift toward greater presence and joy as you let yourself relax and enjoy your Essence now. Recognize that this shift is part of a planetary wave of evolution. While it is immensely simple to explain, we know it is not always so easy to put into practice or to maintain. Recognize that it is a process of coming back, again and again. Each time, returning is easier and time away more brief.

This is a process of trust that is more about trusting your Soul and allowing your life to be in, of, and for God/Goddess, the One All That Is. This is a level of surrender that is truly delicious and magical, once you allow it to be. As you all learn to relax and trust yourselves, your Souls are calling to your destiny. This is a long-awaited project. We are all delighted to see it manifesting in life the way it is.

We are lightened by your shifts and progress, and feel you are well on your way to the expansions you have been requesting. Relax and trust that it is all working in Divine timing. As you relax, you come into alignment with this timing. So it cannot happen any happier or faster than it is. Everything is perfect, including the unfolding of your life. So allow yourself to have that. Revel in the bliss and joy of this deepest surrender. You are powerfully loved and held, and nothing could deter you from that. All is well. Now go in joy/enjoy.

Wishes and Dreams

The writing was flowing smoothly. I was more consistently engaged in the practices Magdalene was sharing and integrating her teachings as they applied in my life. Sometimes her guidance seemed to come out of nowhere, and appeared unconnected with anything I was conscious of. Yet her guidance was usually relevant and timely, even when I did not see it in the moment. This was one of those days.

Mary Magdalene: Today we are interested in speaking with you about dreams and wishes, the differences therein and their virtues. Dreams *are those things (and experiences) that you are inspired to create, while* wishes *are things you* hope *for and would like to happen. Let us explain further.*

A dream *is a deeply seeded desire. It is a plan that you hold in your heart, though you may not recognize it as such. It is often vague and specific at the same time. It has a certain feeling-tone or quality.*

Wishes are hopes; they have no grounding in the heart-seed. While full of heartfelt intent, a wish does not have the quality of being or presence that a dream has. It is a nice idea. It is something you hope for.

Be aware, when you are verbalizing to others, of your wishes/hopes versus dreams (your inborn intentions). Recognize that they may look or sound the same. But they do not feel the same, nor do they have the same quality. A dream has a strong quality of light, while a hope or wish has light building within it.

You have dreams and hopes, and they are not to be confused. Allow both to grow, but do not distract your dreams with your hopes. Hopes (wishes) are delights of the heart, but they do not carry the force-field that is embodied in the heart of your dream.

While these seem like picky, even petty esoteric distinctions, allow yourself the luxury of this new awareness. Let yourself notice the differences, and you may be surprised yourself at how easily one can become distracted with wishes and forget focusing on dreams. That is all for now.

The Practice: Heart Dream Meditation

1. Start to notice your cravings and longings. Identify your dreams and your hopes or wishes. Review your intentions (developed earlier in Roll Out the Red Carpet, page 167) to identify which category these desires fall under. None are wrong, just different.

   - Dreams come from a deeper heart place and are often connected to Soul intention and destiny.

   - Wishes (or hopes) are often lighter in quality, more superficial, and can be a distraction from your deeper desires. They can also come from the dominant culture and media.

   Discern the difference (or make your best guess) so you can place your attention and intention where you prefer. This distinction allows you choice, which brings freedom and power.

2. Sit in a quiet spot, where you can be undisturbed for 15 minutes or longer. Create sacred space for yourself with candles, incense, and music or using any of your favorite methods. (Or try something new!)

3. Breathe deeply. Relax, settle, and center, using any of the meditations in this book, or any that are part of your practice. Feel your body rested and relaxed, your feet connected to the earth through the floor.

4. After several minutes, allow your attention to float gently to the center of your chest, to your heart. Feel, sense, or imagine your heart-center. Notice the color, shape, texture, temperature, etc. of your heart's terrain.

5. Discover the chambers of your heart. Your heart has many rooms, each holding different treasures. Explore these rooms.

6. Allow yourself to travel to the place where your deep dreams and holy desires reside. Using as many senses as you can, note what this room looks and feels like.

7. Ask to be shown your dreams. Ask your Holy Desire to present itself. There may be one or many. They may be old and familiar or completely unexpected. Feel, sense, or imagine them as completely as you can. Receive whatever you are shown openly.

   - If the images or sensations you receive are confusing or unclear, ask, "How does this relate to _____ (my dreams, desires, work, home, relationship, family, etc.)?"

   - You can always ask clarifying questions to make the answers more understandable. If the images or answers are still unclear, trust that they will reveal themselves when it is time.

8. Be sure to take a few moments to fully return to your waking consciousness. Breathe deeply several times. Wiggle your fingers and toes. Open your eyes and stretch.

9. Take notes in your journal or sketch a drawing so that you are able to capture as much of this as possible. This guidance fades quickly.

Blessing in Disguise

Mary Magdalene: Greetings dear. Tonight we wish to speak on change and fear, two topics that are in the minds and hearts of many, including yourself. Fear is a big topic, and there is much we can and will say. But tonight we wish to start by addressing the underlayment of fear: disconnection from Source.

Early in the plan design (the experiment of humanity as it is), it was decided that those who would come to earth would have "amnesia" of sorts regarding their past—all manner of previous life experiences.

This was intended as a blessing, as awareness of life's previous entanglements (positive or negative) with others can be a burden. This lack of awareness keeps one from knowledge of one's participation in so-called negative or positive life events. This disengagement from previous times allows everyone free will to choose and be in the current life expression more fully. This is obvious.

What is also perhaps obvious is that in one's current lifetime, having awareness of previous events (history) can be a tremendous burden. The desire to repair that damage can be a blessing and a curse. The blessing is that, in the desire to right a wrong, a good deed can be done. The disadvantage (not really a curse) is that, without the full picture of that life event, carrying only the memory of one's own participation, further damage can be done.

Sometimes an event or experience that seems to be "bad" has an excellent outcome or benefit for that individual or others. Paradoxically, sometimes a good deed has unintended negative side-effects. Thus, the lack of knowledge of one's previous incarnational entanglements has its advantages.

The disadvantages are equally obvious. Without knowledge of good and bad outcome, one has no way to know what effects one has on the whole. Through errors in judgment, laziness, misunderstanding, greed, or anger, one can unwittingly harm another without even ever knowing it. It can be devastating to have that knowledge and devastating NOT to.

The main challenge we see for humans at this time is to create more awareness and connection to Spirit, so that the disconnection is not so great. So many lives are wasted pursuing frivolous ego pursuits. While it is a free-will environment and nothing is truly lost, many are also waking up to see the disadvantage and inherent emptiness in this.

Disconnection is Illusion

One of the side effects is fear. The fear most feel is a result of disconnection from Spirit, or a perception of such. Disconnection from Spirit, however, implies a state that is an illusion. It assumes you are separate, and therefore connected or disconnected. This is farthest from truth.

You can see evidence of this when you feel lost and confused about the direction or turns your life is taking. Even in a fairly high-consciousness, high-success lifestyle you may feel at times that things are not going right. You can think you do not have enough work, your relationship is a struggle, your social life is lacking, or you have business or financial worries.

This is a crisis of connection. You, in those moments, truly forget that you are Spirit in human form, a Goddess living life in Heaven on Planet Earth. You think you are someone who needs to pray to an outside other for help, that you seek an outside other for guidance.

This is illusion; it is all you. You are the Goddess in the form. You are the one you are seeking. There is no you but you.

This is complicated. If there is theft, loss, or harm, you blame another. Or you blame yourself for being out of harmony or in negative vibration with the event that occurred. You criticize yourself, for if you experience that reality, you created the experience. Then you feel you need to get into a better vibration or "headspace" in order for the experience to shift. This is still ego seeking to change ego!

So what needs to happen instead? Recognize that this is all God/Goddess. All of it! Even you upset is God. Burst frozen plumbing pipes, lost job, speeding ticket, or missed appointments are all the perfection of God. There is no need to judge the event as bad. You would be doing so from the VERY limited vantage point of your current time/space reality. This is so limited. We cannot convey this enough.

When the difficult event happens, love it. As God, being Goddess, just love it. Trust that it is Spirit and that everything is okay. We do not mean to not act; still take the actions needed in the moment to call the plumber, look for a job, or whatever else is called for. But also trust 100% that it is "all good and all Goddess" happening to you, through you, and for you. That is your intention and prayer, that is Heaven on Planet Earth, is it not?

Facets of Fear

Life is unfolding exactly as it needs to. It does not always appear this way. We understand that frustration. The obsession with rising to judgment is just habit. You have 5,000 years of bad habit and conditioning. They are being undone brick by brick.

The fear we spoke of earlier is a byproduct of your perceived disconnection, which is a byproduct of forgetting. This is part of the agreed-upon program, decided upon by the Elohim, the Gods and Goddesses of Light. (Hint: they are you!) The creation team oversight committee (angels or whatever you wish to call the team captains) developed the game or experiment that you agreed to. When you come to understand it fully, you will be surprised at the simplicity and the elegance to the design.

The other facet of the fear, from the beginning, has been an element of control. Early on in the experiment of masculine power, several thousand years ago, those in power wished to keep things this way. The separation and disconnection from the Divine Essence Self (you as Goddess Spirit) furthered their goals to keep you in the game of ego, access, acquisition, and desires.

You are easily swayed as a people. Material needs became a priority when spiritual values were forgotten or lost. It is indeed a grave sadness that this control often came from those in power spiritually, but that is the case. They, too, had forgotten, as a result of being active playing members of the game.

Choice Point

This is the challenge: those who designed the game played it also. They became fully engrossed in the rules and design. In other words, as players they forgot, too! They overlooked the fact that they are not separate from the game, failing to recall that there ever was another version of reality.

This forgotten connection to (and as) Spirit is a fundamental error in the experiment design. It has created all manner of destruction, to the point that life on your heavenly planet home is in grave danger. As we mentioned earlier, there were reasons for those choices. This was not a mistake. We are seeing how it is playing out many eons down the line.

The choice point is now. It is an interesting time to be alive, for you have the chance to awaken to that connection and recollection that we are all Spirit alive in human (and non-human) form. You are given a huge opportunity. If you choose, you can soar and fly.

Your mission is to awaken humanity to the presence of the Divine in everything. While you do not see how to do this, recognize that but you are not the only one with this mission. Realize is that you have more skill, and a greater team in play, than you are currently aware.

You Are God

We are here to tell you that the time is ripe. It is now and it is good. Connect them to Source in whatever form they know it. Remind them that they are good, they are God, and they are to recognize (re-cognize: to think again) their God selves.

They are not actually disconnected, for if they were truly disconnected they would be dead. The disconnection is like a blanket over a TV that is on. It is still on, getting signal and shining out a show. But no one sees it if there is a blanket on it. You are advised to take the blanket off and to show others how to do so. Lift off the veils of illusion about who you all truly are. We start with you and we start now. Thank you for Listening. For tonight we are complete.

This Divine Download felt more like a transmission. It was so meaty and with so much to digest. As I re-read what Magdalene shared, I saw deeper layers and levels of meaning. Such juicy complexity and simplicity at the same time. I felt pure awe and honor at being gifted the opportunity to delve into these insights, exploring and applying them in my life.

Creating HOPE

It was a lovely, blustery autumn Thanksgiving day, with deep blue skies and rain clouds threatening overhead. This quotation crossed my awareness: "The grateful Soul is content with all she sees, while the complaining Soul is discontent in the midst of paradise." (*source unknown*) I had so much to be grateful for, yet sometimes I couldn't even see it. While I knew I wasn't unique, it was still embarrassing to admit. It seemed appropriate to spend some time in quiet contemplation of gratitude, and I needed to do it before the day's events got away from me. Wondering what the Magdalene would say, I sat and centered myself quietly. I felt a slight shift and the presence of Magdalene almost immediately. I sensed her words and quickly started to type.

Mary Magdalene: Many of your people desire and are aware of big positive changes coming ahead. As in past eras, there are also those who are urging that the "end times" are coming, and others who see this as a return to the light. Some see this happening "in-body" (occurring on the planet). Still others see this return to the light as signaling the end of the physical form and a return to the spiritual world. They refer to it as "rapture," or "ascension," as if there is a Divine elevator of light that will carry you to "heaven" in physical form to another world beyond this one.

We see all this as nonsense, due to our perspective that your world is Heaven already. Do you not? You are aware that the ways in which you think and feel manifest certain aspects of your reality. The formless of Spirit and Soul become form through the physical world of heart and body. You are a vehicle for manifesting Heaven on planet Earth. You are indeed the ones you have been waiting for, as many have sensed and said.

Heaven on Planet Earth

Similarly, you are the ones to bring the Heaven-like life that you feel, sense, and desire into the 3-D manifestations of reality. As you do this, you bring more light through you. This conveyance of light is literally an embodiment of heaven. You are here to embody HOPE: Heaven on Planet Earth. Show them the way.

Claire: Oh, HOPE! I like that! And how do I do this? I see/feel/sense this as Truth, and yet…I don't feel I embody this. Often I am aware that this is Heaven on Planet Earth, as a conceptual framework, an idea and an ideal, but it's not my day-to-day experience.

Mary Magdalene: Well, certainly not yet. You are a Goddess-in-Training, a Priestess from past and future. Yours is to practice and teach from that practice. This is what makes the exercise such a delight: as you learn, you teach and others grow, too.

Claire: Delightful! So what about my mind's critical display, when I see garbage on the street, violence or poverty? I automatically think, "This is not Heaven on Earth." How do I deal with that?

Mary Magdalene: Just be with the practice first. We will advise you. First, fully love what you have, as well as you are able. Trust that, as you love what you have, more of that joy flows through you.

It is no coincidence that, on this day of giving-thanks, that the message of gratitude would be the place we essentially begin. Seeing, feeling, sensing, and loving the heaven you have created for yourself (in partnership with all life, seen and unseen) will flow more of that goodness to you. It is a difficult concept to convey intellectually, and this is why we start with PRACTICE.

Be the joy you wish to teach, and they will naturally seek you for more. This is simple math. Do your side of the equation. This is the first aspect of your practice and message. We love you and are delighted to serve with you and through you. You are made for this.

This message (and the practice that emerged out of it, below), were the most impactful and life altering. I return to this practice and perspective continually and the gifts from it are deeper with the progression of time.

The Practice: Creating Heaven on Planet Earth

The steps and process are simple, yet not always so easy. This practice is surprisingly quite profound. It works best when woven into daily moments quite fluidly, rather than while formally sitting and "doing" it.

1. Notice, feel, and enjoy the perfection of this time and place, in the moment you are experiencing it. You can only start from your current vantage point.

2. Feel, think, and exude the fact that this IS *Heaven on Planet Earth*. When an event, issue, or experience occurs, take a moment to breathe, ground, and center. Acknowledge that this is Heaven on Planet Earth.

3. At times, your viewpoint may seem quite the contrary to your ideal (and you have many examples leaping into your mind, no doubt). Observe how the mind may want to change, disapprove, or criticize what is and what is not. This resistance

to appreciating your present life experience is a natural barrier to actually entering the kingdom of God, Heaven on Planet Earth. Your current experience is your point of attraction, the starting place for the version of Heaven you seek to manifest. Your Soul calls this forth. Bless the moment.

4. Shine. The primary task is to be and convey the light. Always remember the light and the joy of the God spark that you are bearing and bestowing.

5. As you do this, your vibration will naturally rise and your point of attraction will shift to match this. Those people, things, and experiences that are NOT aligned with Heaven on Planet Earth will begin to shift, fade, or generally remove themselves from your sphere of awareness.

6. As best you can, hold the awareness of HOPE in your consciousness at all times. By knowing this, you will begin to create and embody more ideal life experiences. There is great work to be done here in partnership with the unseen world and Divine helpers (co-creating via prayer), but for now focus here. So the practice is just that: practice.

Emerge © 2014 Claire Sierra

Chapter 7

Tools for the Path

Primary Practices

Throughout the process of *Listening*, Magdalene indicated certain skills and tools that support Feminine Soul emerging. Many of these wove into the insights of her Divine Downloads. There were others that fit into a unique basket, which she shares here.

Mary Magdalene: Today we wish to address the manner and style in which you may choose to activate the awakening of the Divine Feminine in yourself and then (naturally) in others. There are practices that are relevant to convey. We wish to outline the primary tools to develop the inner experience of the Divine in feminine form. Many have been discussed previously in this guidebook. Others will be developed in this next section.

- *Mind Work: Healing thoughts, intention, and beliefs which connect you to a deeper source of wisdom and guidance.*

- *Ritual: Practices that bring you in connection with Divine.*

- *Prayer/Sitting Meditation: Deep listening and receptivity processes.*

- *Guided Imagery/Breathwork: Imaginal relationship with Soul and self.*

- *Art/Movement/Dance: Sacred beauty, flow and connection to Source through creative acts.*

- *Light and Love: Directing God/Source energy to self or others for healing.*

As we mentioned, many of these have been shared already. There are a few we wish to elaborate on that have not yet been discussed.

Light and Love

Mary Magdalene: Today we wish to speak to you of the love and light that are available to you all right now. It has always been, but the quantity and quality of the light and its refined nature are more tangible, more liquid, and more luminescent.

We wish to guide you now to the use of this light and how you can develop this as a force of healing, far beyond that which is currently recognized in your culture.

The Way of the Mari, the Magdalene Path, is the Way of Light. This light is love manifest into form. What this means for you and those you teach is that you can begin to cultivate this as a direct force of healing. The means to do this is simple and merely takes Awareness, Recollection, *and* Intention.

Awareness *is the knowledge of the power of this light and its healing force. Just know it exists and waits to be used. It is a generative power that can be developed by those of any station, culture, or means. It knows no bounds or limits, and integrates all.*

With the awareness *then comes* recollection *or* remembrance. Remember *to use it,* remember *the power and the skill, and then apply it through* intention. Intention *is the direction you face to convey the light. In other words, this intention is the map* and *the arrow. You point it and it goes. This is so simple. We have spoken about this earlier, so for now, start with this.*

The Practice: Prayer Beads

One way your light and intention can be focused and directed is through the use of prayer beads. Prayer settles and stills us, so that we can hear the whispers of the Divine and remember who we really are. In that relaxed and open awareness our intentions are carried to Spirit into manifestation. One simple and relaxing method is using prayer beads, which are part of many spiritual traditions. Many are familiar with mala and rosary beads, from the Hindu, Buddhist and Catholic faiths. Mala beads have 108 beads, said to be for each of the sacred names of God. Rosary beads, coincidentally or intentionally, have 54 beads. Thus by repeating 2 "rounds" you can equal that same sacred number. Each is used to deeply resonate with a repetitive prayer, chant or mantra. (A mantra is a holy or special phrase that is repeated over and over.)

1. Sit quietly and focus on your day and current life experience. What good are you intending to draw to you? What challenges could you use support with?

2. Develop or choose a mantra, or prayer. Or allow an affirmation or special phrase to come to you that supports your intention. Reciting a sacred name of God is very powerful. Some other examples are: Om Mani Padme Hum, or Aum (from Buddhism), Hail Mary Full of Grace, the Spirit is with You (from the Christian Tradition), or I am the light and love of the Divine, all else is illusion (an affirmations that I love).

3. Hold your rosary or mala beads in your hands. Say your chosen prayer, mantra, sacred phrase or affirmation while holding each bead. Move beads between each prayer.

Prayer Power

I pondered the impact of Awareness, Recollection and Intention and saw how this impacted my life. I wondered how this related to Love and Light as tools for healing. So I centered myself one morning and opened myself to receive Magdalene's message. She came immediately.

Mary Magdalene: We wish to talk to you about the healing power of love and prayer. This is a simple practice to convey, but one that takes lifetimes to fully appreciate and possess. The simplicity makes it often overlooked, as well. We shall summarize to say that the practice of using Love and Light was the highest order of healing in our ministry, The Way. The manner in which we each practiced it was fairly individualized, and yet the common threads were the same.

This is similar to the practice that Yeshua and I used (which he spoke of earlier), bridging with healing and light to one in need. This, however, can be accomplished by one or many. It is amplified with more participants, but that is not always practical. The underlying dynamic is that thoughts and feelings create bridges between one and the intended, whether human or otherwise. Notice that when you care for another, you often feel connected. That is because it is actually so, from a quantum perspective.

So when one person thinks of another, a light bridge or energy thread is passed from one to the other. This can be used for good or ill. There is actually a string or cord of light that connects you when you are intending thoughts of healing or negativity for another.

When you have the intent to help or heal, there is an exponential force that is a booster adding to that field. This comes from your feelings. So our advice is to heighten your awareness of thoughts of good or ill especially toward another. Why hurt or cause pain, when you can help or heal instead? Using this simple practice, send your thoughts and feelings of love and good-will toward your intended, be they sick or unwell in body, mind, or spirit.

The Practice: Energy Bridge

1. Identify a person (or animal or place) in need that you wish to send healing thoughts and prayers. Inwardly ask their Soul or higher self if they are willing to receive this energy blessing. If you sense, feel, or hear a "yes," proceed. If not, why bother? It would be energy sent and spent in waste.

2. After determining a "yes," then bring their image or energy/sense impression into your heart-space. Feel, sense, or imagine them in full detail as you know them to be. Feel a light or cord from your heart to theirs. The light bridge connection is made.

3. Visualize your friend in full health: robust, happy, vibrant and whole. Surround her with the goodness of your vision and intentions. Activate your heart's care, bathing them in the rays of your love and delight. Allow that love-feeling to grow and expand.

4. Some like to infuse prayers into this field, whether they are memorized from sacred text, phrases of comfort toward the intended recipient, or speaking from the heart directly to the Divine. Use mala or prayer beads as described previously, if you wish. Embracing these words of healing can create alignment for some. This is optional, however, since it is not the words themselves that are magical, but the intention of the one who prays. There is not any special force behind the prayer-words

themselves. The Divine is not looking for some special phrase, like magical faerie dust, to open the key to the secret kingdom of health and well-being. Your heart's open and pure intent is prayer enough.

5. After a few minutes (or as long as you are able to maintain concentration), consciously sever the cord of connection. Release your intended receiver and bring your awareness back to yourself: your body and surroundings. Your ability to focus and maintain this energy will get longer with practice.

6. Breathe for a few moments. Get grounded back into your own time-space reality. Know that you have helped the recipient immensely.

Candle Magic

Mary Magdalene: Today we wish to share about the ritual practice of candle magic. We sense some nervous trepidation about using this term "magic," with the connection to witchcraft, past lives burned at the stake, and so forth. And yet what is magic? It's not abracadabra (poof!), but the art of changing consciousness at will. Cast off the old baggage and see how it is now irrelevant to your current experience. Indeed, many of you desire more *magic, not less. And ritual is merely making sacred space for the Divine to come play—conscious creation at its finest. So we thought best to elaborate so that you can relax in understanding about this high art.*

First, we must speak of candles. Bringers of light and heat for many generations are now relegated to mere home decoration. Still, you cannot help but notice how many are offered for purchase and how women, especially, are drawn to candles. Yes, there is something special about this quality of light, and we shall speak of this.

Something is overlooked about the light of candles. It harkens back to a time in humanity when this was the only "artificial" non-sunlight available. This was a tremendous step forward in the development of humanity, for the days did not end with the dipping of the sun below the horizon and could be stretched. Candles were rare and expensive, as high "technology" (such as it was), and were used sparingly. They were for special occasions initially, rather than daily use. We see this practice carried over into modern times. This is disappointing, for there is something special and magical about the quality of this light.

Candles, as with fire, are pure expression of Source into form. You come from this light, as the star that you are. At the core of your planet there is fire. Your sun is fire. This fire is inside you, also. It is your Spirit and what keeps you moving in form, with the vehicle of your body.

Thus, there is an elemental quality to candlelight. A small, contained fire sits before you. This fire helps recollect the fire of your Soul and Spirit, coming from Source essence. This is the essence of Candle Magic.

When you light candles and see them before you, you feel the magic of light. Where is this small fire coming from? How does it come into being on your table? There is mystery there, and it is overlooked as commonplace.

We encourage you to light candles daily, as part of your morning practices or throughout your day. With the lighting of each candle, take a moment to breathe. Speak or think an intention for your day and your world, near and far. Allow yourself a sacred moment to pray and give thanks for all you are, all you have, and all you dream of being.

Spark of Awareness

If you are feeling resistance to this practice, it may be connected to the name only and comes from deep in the psyche. There was a dark period in history when the practice of anything deemed "magical" was dangerous and ill-advised. Magic and witchcraft became associated with the work of the devil. This powerful art was obliterated by those who did not wish for power to be in the hands of the people. We wish to share some history, for context.

For many generations, these practices we share were well known and quite commonplace. One of these areas was southern France and northern Italy, where I, The Magdalene and the other Mari priestesses traveled. Here my memory is well established and quite obviously venerated. In these and other lands, there were those with direct knowledge of ways that connected one to self and Source.

In the south of France, our people became known as the Cathars, meaning "pure ones." The purity does not refer to their lifestyle or ascetic practices, as some have incorrectly assumed. The purity refers to the lineage of teachings and the way they held the practices of Yeshua ben Joseph, the Christos of Judea, your Jesus Christ.

In these regions, there was open knowledge of these rituals. They were not held solely by the Cathars (or Cathari), but also in the Northern lands (what is now Scandinavia, northern Europe, and the U.K.), where ways of Earth and Spirit were closely practiced for centuries. These peoples experienced direct connection with God, in whatever form or name they used. They observed reverence for all life and knew the blessings of daily communion with Source, Soul, self, and sisters. There was peace and harmony in the land and community. Men and women lived and practiced together without hierarchy. Their cultures honored life as sacred and knew the balance was to be held lovingly by each of us. They understood the power of prayer, intention, and gratitude.

You may be surprised, believing these to be newer concepts of common consciousness, and in some places they are. But trust and believe that these ideas are as old as time, which is why Jesus/Yeshua came to all who had ears to hear him.

In time, the power structures of spirituality turned into religion, and the men forgot the role and value of the women in spiritual leadership. There is a natural tendency for those in power to crave more. So while well intended, those in leadership became corrupted by greed for power, possessions, and influence. They decided, and then came to believe, that it was "God's will" to kill those who were outside the belief frame they held. They forgot there is truly only one God but many paths to serve and love this One Source.

With this belief and power shift came the Crusades and Inquisition — the mass slaughter of almost a million (some say) who did not believe as the Holy Roman (Catholic) Church dictated as the only true faith.

Any outspoken or unique individual was at risk to be accused of practicing witchcraft, which carried a sentence of death, often after torture. This accomplished the silencing of women. "Witchcraft" is the name the church devised for those who practiced "the Old Ways." The Old Religion of the Goddess, honored self, nature, and community while living in harmony and balance with all creation, as had been practiced for centuries.

Healers (women and men) used local herbs and simple cures as medicine, for eons. The church vilified these practices, labeling them Satan worship. This was farthest from the truth. While not all "simples" were helpful, many were. This home-based healing was a threat to the growing power structure of academia, which was blossoming out of religious institutions. Medicine, taught in universities only open to men, was based on a Greek style of philosophy and healing, which was not endearing of women as a gender.

We digress here, but it is important for the discussion of Candle Magic. The fear and hesitation about using these words comes from a time when it would be deadly for you to appear to engage these traditions even slightly. These times are over, and this embodied fear of retribution and attack must be released so that women can claim their voice and power.

Indeed, it is important that these ways be brought from the dark closet to the light of day, to be reclaimed as commonplace and used by all. As this occurs in so many lands, the strength of the One Holy Church wanes. The rebirth of indigenous spiritual traditions arises. This is indigenous as in instinctive, native, inborn, and natural, emerging from and in relation to Spirit.

Let this spark of flame — candle flickers — be an inspiration to others so that this ritual of peace spreads like a wildfire of the spirit! Know that as you re-engage these traditions, you are mindful and sage in their use, so that no harm comes to your Temple Home or Office.

The Practice: Candle Magic

Light candles daily. This is a simple ritual practice that triggers your deep, instinctual, unconscious self. It is a nudge from your Soul that says "pay attention, something different is happening." Your *attention* can serve your *intention*. This practice reminds you to make every day special, as every day is sacred. All this comes from the spark of a match and the lighting of a small flame. Such a simple pleasure.

1. With each act of lighting a candle, take a moment to create a blessing or affirmation. Here you may intend your hopes and dreams for your day and beyond. Tune into your thoughts, feelings, and body sensations. Be spontaneous and brief.

2. As you create affirmations and intentions for yourself, you may naturally think of others you care about. Say prayers and blessings for those beloveds who are ill, in need, or less fortunate.

3. Finally, you have an ideal moment to practice gratitude. Count your blessings. See, feel, and sense how blessed you already are. Appreciate your life. Notice how this thinking uplifts your heart and spirit to joy.

4. Be careful not to leave flames untended. We do not want to create wildfire, except of the Spirit!

LightBreath Meditation

Mary Magdalene: There are several meditation skills we have alluded to that we wish to teach. The first is the LightBreath Meditation you used recently and long ago. This is one of many we will offer you to use. This is not new to you, but we promise this is an excellent and powerful tool for clearing effluent from the vehicle. The body is the vehicle for the Spirit in form, and keeping that clean and clear is of paramount importance.

We encourage you to use this one often. Delight in the partnership with the light, for it is alive and conscious — far more so than you currently realize. We wish you well, and for tonight we are complete.

The Practice: LightBreath Meditation

This is a powerful meditation that guides and implants light directly into the body, exactly where it is needed, regardless of the conscious awareness of the user. When you practice LightBreath Meditation, you do not need to know precisely where it is needed. The light knows and it will go there. Certainly you can connect and direct it, but the light is God or Source, and therefore has an intelligence of its own. It goes where the recipient needs it, regardless of her awareness of this need.

*For a free audio recording of this meditation, go to BlissBreakthrough.com or MagdalenePath.com. An MP3 recording is available for download by entering your name and email address in the box. Also look for the Free Resources tab.

The meditation goes like this:

1. Settle yourself into your chair, taking a few moments to get comfortable where you are now. Turn off any electronic devices or other distractions so that you are not disturbed for 10-20 minutes.

2. Gently close your eyes, if you are in a place where it's safe to do so. (Eventually you can do this with eyes open, for equally great benefit.)

3. Begin by gently noticing the breath, not changing it or forcing anything, just noticing. As you bring awareness to the breath, you will notice that it deepens naturally, without effort or force. As you do this, allow your energy to settle and pool, with calm serenity. Take several minutes to relax and open the breath in this easy manner.

4. Invite the presence of The Magdalene and the Mari priestesses, for guidance and protection. Include any other deities or aspects of the Divine you feel most aligned and connected to.

5. Call the light in the following manner. Focus on the spot at the top of your head. Feel, sense, or imagine this spot spinning open, like the aperture of a camera or unfurling like a flower. As it opens, invite the light from the universal sun. The light will appear, often with force, for it wants to be used and sits waiting otherwise. At this calling, the warm, liquid, golden-white light will begin to stream forth into your head, where it can swirl and move easily. This light will shimmer and sparkle, swirl and dance. It may glide like a warm river of liquid honey light.

6. Focus on receiving this liquid light into your head: your brain, eyes, ears, and third eye. This is likely to happen for some time. Use your breath to direct the light. On the in-breath, let the light come in, and on the out-breath make a conscious choice to release whatever no longer serves you.

7. Draw the light down into your body, settling into your heart, neck, and chest. As the light enters and flows through your body, it naturally displaces and clears anything ready to be released. Intend the light toward any muscles that are sore or to other body parts that are known to have difficulties, injuries, or ailments.

8. Let this light swirl and cycle through your body for several minutes, as long as you can maintain concentration. When you lose focus, gently bring your attention back to your breath and the cycle of light moving within you.

9. Allow the light to move out of your body with your breath. Send it through your feet, deep into the earth. There it can be received, reclaimed, and recycled, without harm to anyone, for the best and highest of all concerned. This release will happen naturally. With the light and love of conscious awareness, the effects will be more powerful and palpable.

10. Know that if you lose focus, this light is still going where it is needed. Once activated, this LightBreath has intelligence and is healing and expanding your being in alignment with your Soul contract.

11. When you are ready to finish, or you sense that this session is complete, begin this closure process. From this expanded place of awareness, first give thanks. Activate your gratitude. Appreciate yourself for taking this time and allowing yourself this experience. Give thanks to all your Divine guides, guardians, and teachers who brought you to this moment so exquisitely. Thank Mary Magdalene, the Mari priestesses, and any other Divine beings or deities who came to work with you today. Finally, give gratitude to this infinite intelligence of light, which is love, Source, God, and All There Is.

12. Relax and breathe for a few moments while your eyes are still closed. Allow yourself to enjoy this new, clear state of awareness before jumping into the next adventure of your Divine life.

Accessing God Connection

After several months of using the LightBreath meditation practice with myself and clients, I awoke after a dream that implanted the idea of a God connection, like a phone line to Source. I knew that if I was alive, I had a Spirit connection, but it did not always feel "on" or live. This created a new awareness in me that I felt deeply grateful for, as I discovered it was something I could initiate! Magdalene then followed up in her teaching:

Mary Magdalene: Today you awoke with a new concept: the "God Line." Rather like a phone line between you and Source, the God Line is the string of light that connects you to Spirit in God/Goddess form. You have known that your blessing is to awaken connection to the Divine for others, yet you have not known how exactly this is achieved. You have had a sense that meditation, energy work, and guided imagery play a role. This morning, you received a more tangible sense of how that actually works — a physical representation.

This glowing cord of light connects each of you to the Divine. It gets severed at the moment of death to discontinue the life energy flowing to your body. Some have a larger, more intentional God Line than others. For some it is a narrow, tattered string. You can never tell when looking at someone what the state of their God Line is. There are those you would never suspect who have a thick, juicy, well-developed God Line, and you might think they are heathen, selfish, greedy bastards (pardon our crudeness).

Show people the way to connect to God. This can be done in a variety of manners: prayer, meditation, intention, or request. There are many forms for these basic methods, through guided visualization, making art, being in nature, exercising, dancing, chanting, drumming, or playing music.

What you may notice in all of these is that some degree of activity or intention is required. These are all creative outlets. There is no passive connection to the God line—though there can be unconscious connection, as is obvious in those without spiritual inclination who are still living and breathing life.

So your job, as a "teacher of God," is to help people make the connection consciously themselves so that they feel relaxed, alert, and aware of it while it is occurring. Creating connection with Source, Self, and Soul is perhaps the most important thing that you do. And you do it over and over, sometimes without conscious awareness. So here is a tool for this connection. Share this with others. Amen.

The Practice: Open Your God Line

The awareness of the God Line is a tool to engage. The method is quite simple, and with practice can be done in seconds, regardless of the outer circumstances present in your life. This practice activates a glowing cord of light that connects you to the Divine. Your God Line gets initiated at birth to start the flow of life energy to you, stopping at death to as this same life energy ceases.

1. First, relax into your breath. This aligns you with your Self. As an aspect of God, you must be in alignment with yourself in order to increase the connection to God. (This word can be used interchangeably with Source, Spirit, All That Is, Oneness, Christ, Goddess, etc.)

2. From this place, become grounded and centered, which is important for clear connection to God. Breath awareness allows you to receive God Essence on the in-breath and release on the out-breath.

3. Next, on your exhale, release pain, frustration, and toxins of any kind — physical, mental, or emotional. Release them down your feet into the Earth mother, who can purify and regenerate this energy. This enhances presence and relaxed connection with your Soul Self.

4. Become aware of your God Line. Allow your attention to go to the top of your head (also known as the crown chakra). See, feel, or sense this space opening, spinning like a camera aperture or unfolding like a flower. (Alternatively, some feel this connection best by opening though the heart chakra in the middle of the chest. That is fine, too.) See, feel, or sense a line or tube of light flowing from the heavens into your head or heart. This may be a thin, fine gossamer string; a large, thick pipe; or something else entirely. It glows softly or brightly with silvery-golden iridescent light, a brilliant and refined color that can be difficult to describe.

5. Bring this light into your body, filling the vessel of your Self like a vase or basket. If you see any places where the light may be oozing or leaking out, create a patch with that same light. Notice that the light in the container begins to grow and brighten, as if you are filling a jar (though it may not be from bottom up).

6. Receive and contain this light. Allow yourself to let it in. Send the light to areas of your body that need nourishment, rejuvenation, and healing. Notice how it goes to areas that are hurt or ill. Allow the vessel of the body to absorb this like a dry sponge in the parched desert.

7. After several minutes, complete the process with gratitude. Before you go about your day, take a moment to give thanks to the Source of this light and life. Thank yourself for tending to you in this nurturing manner.

8. You do not need to sever this connection (it is always there), but as your awareness shifts, you can open your eyes. Practice feeling the God Line with your eyes open. Fill your vessel with light through the top of your head or feet as you go through your daily activities. Notice times when your energy is low or you feel overwhelmed or frustrated. See if this creates more energy or a better mood. It probably will.

Golden Orb of Light

My life was full of incredible connections and synchronicity. I'd had a powerful Akashic Records channeling session with my friend Tomar. I was asking her about the book and who it was meant to serve, so I could get the message to those who needed it. She mentioned a golden orb of light that she saw me using in healing sessions with people. She suggested I ask Magdalene about it, which led to an incredible communication and transmission. Magdalene addressed another question on my heart/mind and then led me into a breathtaking experience.

Claire: Magdalene, please share with me about the golden orb of light. And can you induct me into an experience of this golden orb?

Mary Magdalene: Yes, certainly, though first we wish to speak about the High Priestess Training you've been pondering. This, my dear, is what you already are; you do not need another to tell you so. You already lead others as High Priestess and are meant to do so, in this there is no argument. You are a peer and collaborateur, meant to give gifts to share with her group. While it may satisfy your ego to have this outward acknowledgement, recognize that this is who you are already. Know this is so, and step into your own spiritual authority.

Claire: Okay, thanks. That clears that up.

Mary Magdalene: Now, about the golden orb. This is the body of work you are meant to impart. You carry this orb in your body, in your womb. It is why you have not birthed another being; this is your golden child. Note that Magdalene (myself) is often depicted with eggs or golden orbs.

Claire: Yes, I'm seeing flashes of images, like the Black Madonna and child that are so venerated at Montserrat in Spain and Chartres in France.

Mary Magdalene: Yes. And there are others. Close your eyes and allow this golden orb to descend, encompassing your head and heart. Let it settle there and expand. Now embrace its gentle aura; allow it to infuse your whole field. See, feel, sense, or imagine the golden light coming out your pores. You are shining out radiant, effusive light. Keep aligned with the golden-warm, liquid-honeyed light. This is the state we want you to be living in more and more, and especially when you work with others, and when connected to the book-creating process.

Claire: Wow, amazing. I feel it: so soft, yet strong and palpable. Is this connected to energy healing methods I've been trained in? It feels different, though.

Mary Magdalene: You are correct in your understanding. This mystery has been lost in the Western traditions, though not entirely; consider Jesus' ministry and the Laying on of Hands in the Christian tradition. Nonetheless, the Eastern streams of spirituality have retained this as a healing modality. From this tradition, many Western seekers have connected and integrated this into their own practice.

Claire: Fabulous, yes. Is there a way for me to integrate and teach this to others? Or am I to transmit this energy myself?

Mary Magdalene: Yes, work with this; it is embedded in the material in the book (look again more closely). You will surely find it slightly disguised in the GodLine process as well as the LightBreath meditation, and similarly in the teaching from Yeshua about healing. You can add this and build into those pieces, as you wish. We would be delighted with that upgrade and clarification.

Claire: Is this something you use with Jesus?

Mary Magdalene: Yes, it is the foundation with which we teach and heal others.

Claire: Is this something for me to offer, like an energy treatment or transmission, in my work with others?

Mary Magdalene: Yes, though we encourage you to name it and separate it from other lineages, since this is your guiding path. Continue to work with the golden orb yourself, and see how it evolves as you do. We can speak again on this as need be.

Claire: So, what do you suggest I call this?

Mary Magdalene: Magdalene's Blessing or Magdalene Awakening would work for now. Or Blessing of the Magdalene, if you prefer.

Claire: Oh, I like that. Thank you.

Mary Magdalene: This is a Divine transmission of light for healing, health, wholeness, holiness, and wellness. Stay open at the top and connect with the golden orb; this will all become clear. Before you know it, this practice will be off and running! We are so delighted and excited. We bow to you in gratitude for your faithful serving of this path and message.

Claire: You are SO welcome! I love it!

Magdalene Blessing

A week passed. I was practicing drawing down this golden orb of light. To call it "light" is imprecise; it feels more like honey-gold liquid to me. I found myself using it almost without conscious thought or effort. It just came, and I drew it through me.

I returned to query Magdalene, to see what her guidance was. She quickly turned my attention to this golden orb. She had more she wished to impart about the process as I was using it. I remained in dual awareness as I simultaneously experienced the energy of the orb while I was in dialogue with Magdalene, typing.

Mary Magdalene: Turn your attention again to that golden orb of light. Feel or sense it above you, just above your head. Allow it to drop over and within you. See it displace any debris you have collected or cultivated in your own body, aura, magnetic field, or physical being. Allow it to scan through you.

Claire: I notice it settles over my head and heart. It starts small, like the size of a cantaloupe, and then as it enters my body it grows larger. But it never moves beyond my head, chest, and solar plexus.

Mary Magdalene: Yes, that is so. It is bright and light, like warm, liquid, honey gold.

Claire: It feels delicious.

Mary Magdalene: Notice how it balances, harmonizes, and uplifts you, removing all previous negative attachments, thoughts, and worries. Just pure expanded being, that is who you are. We are delighted that you are recalling and reviving this practice, beginning with yourself. Even just short moments are very rejuvenating and healing.

Claire: Now it feels like it is moving down my body more. It feels very trance-like. I'm getting chills up and down my whole body, too.

Mary Magdalene: Yes, it is clearing and cleansing — but likely to remain in the top half of your body (head, heart, chest, and stomach). Then it swooshes down your body, for completion, dragging with it all that is ready to be released into the earth. This is a potent healing tool.

Synchronize your breath. Breathe fully and deeply to support the receiving and releasing that is occurring—especially if you feel emotionally stuck, or physical pressure or energy blockage. This will help any gunk to move through you. Allow the light to grow and glow brighter. Shine the radiance of this golden ball through you, into your whole energy field.

This is a key tool for you to teach, and is an easy and early one to share. It is so opening, centering, and harmonizing, creating a great space for the other tools and processes in this text.

Claire: Wow, that's amazing. Thank you. So where does this go?

Mary Magdalene: In the book, of course, in the section on Tools. These basic skills are crucial for survival and expansion of the human race. Enjoy and indulge often.

Claire: How often should one practice this?

Mary Magdalene: As often as one likes. Ideally, once or twice a day—even in short bursts of a few minutes, as we have done with you now. Morning and evening are ideal, but throughout the workday is excellent also for re-balancing and connection to what is real: Spirit, Source, All That Is. That is reality, the rest is your dream time. Wake up.

Claire: Thank you Magdalene, you are such a great guide to me.

This was an amazing experience among many. To receive her communication and be guided while simultaneously experiencing this energy was exquisite. It has been such a delight to continue this practice and to share it with others.

The Practice: Magdalene Blessing

This energy healing practice comes through the lost arts of the Western mystery tradition, directly related to practices used by Jesus in his healing ministry. It is a Divine transmission of light from Source for health, wholeness, and well-being. As you connect with the golden orb, you may experience pure expanded being, which is who you truly are. Notice how it balances, harmonizes, and uplifts you, removing all previous negative attachments, thoughts, and worries. Practice this energy meditation once or twice a day for several minutes (or longer, if you desire). Even short moments are very rejuvenating and healing. Morning and evening, at waking and before sleep, are best.

1. Close your eyes, relax, and settle yourself for a few minutes. Allow your breath to slow and deepen. Feel your feet on the ground, anchoring you to the planet. Rest in the chair where you sit, or on the bed where you lie, and feel your body open. Relax deeply.

2. Invite Mary Magdalene (and any other Divine guides or helpers you wish) to come with her golden orb into your energetic field.

3. Turn your attention to a golden orb of light, just above your head. Feel or sense it above you. You may see it drop down from the sun, or it may just appear over your head, a few feet (or inches) away.

4. Allow this golden orb to descend, into your head, bathing it with liquid loving light. At first it may be small, often the size of an orange, but you may experience it larger or smaller. Let it drop into into you. It may swirl, pulse or rotate, and should feel very pleasant and relaxing.

5. Embrace its gentle, warm, golden aura. See, feel, sense, or imagine the golden light filling you with effusive, warm, honey-golden light.

6. Let it encompass your heart, then expand or move into your belly, and solar plexus. Notice that it may grow larger as it enters your body. Let it expand and settle there.

7. Allow it to penetrate throughout your whole body, swirling and collecting any tension or toxins as it moves through you. Let it infuse your whole energetic field.

8. Watch it grow until the light is coming through you, out your pores. It will illuminate your whole being, including your energy field.

9. Let it move through and scan you. Notice it displacing any physical, mental, or emotional debris you have collected in your body, aura, or magnetic field. Send or request the golden egg into any areas of pain, injury or illness. Stay aligned with the light as the debris is collected and consumed fully, returning to Oneness.

10. When you feel finished, or the experience naturally starts to complete, the orb-light will return to Source. It may dissipate throughout your body or exit your feet into the ground, or through the top of your head, returning to the heavens.

11. Take a moment to honor and give thanks to Mary Magdalene and the Sisterhood of Light for bringing this tool to you today. Thank any other guides, guardians, Gods, or Goddesses you may feel connected with.

12. Breathe and center yourself for a few moments. Keep your eyes closed, but consciously feel your chair or bed underneath you, becoming aware that you are back in your room. Gently open your eyes, continuing to contain the energy of the experience as much as you are able.

13. Make notes in your journal. Jot down anything you want to retain about the experience, as these tend to fade from memory quickly.

Roles Redefined

As the tools and skills came together, I began to realize all that was within these pages that could be taught and shared with others of like mind and interest. I started to see the potential for programs and trainings, for classes, groups and retreats to explore and master these concepts and skills. As I opened and attuned myself, Magdalene added to my thoughts. She shared her guidance on the inner attitude one needs to hold a position of leadership as one works with others as a healer, teacher, counselor, or guide.

Mary Magdalene: The topic for today is the mindset of a healer and the misperception of the wounded healer archetype. We see this manifesting at large in the world around you. We see this title used as a badge of honor. We wonder how this serves your people, as this does not have to be the case. Alternately, we see the mistaken belief that the healer is a perfected being. This misidentification is equally disruptive and damaging. It ultimately creates discord when the idealized healer, a "guru god" your culture often creates, then falls from the pedestal.

The role of the healer is to bring light and awareness to places in each of us that are hidden. That is the original meaning of the word sin, *hidden or missing the mark; it is an archery term. So one who sins, you see, is not wicked, evil, or full of Satan, as is commonly believed. Instead, one who sins has something missing. That lack or absence creates distress, which begets acting out, which is sin.*

People in sin are hidden from the light, in themselves and in the world around them. The outer world is a manifestation and reflection of the inner world, and vice versa.

The role of healer is vast, regardless of the label you use: doctor, therapist, acupuncturist, massage therapist, nurse. These are all healers. Even those in so-called information services —lawyer, mortgage broker, accountant—they are healers, too. They can bring light in the form of information or services to those in need.

This is a blessing—you are all healers of some sort or another. One acts as a healer when one brings kindness and compassion in service to those who are struggling with a problem—whether that is filling out insurance forms, resolving a health issue, or returning a crushed box of chocolates. Joy and beauty are two powerful gifts. When you look for places to add or increase either (or, better yet, both!) then more healing can happen.

But lose the archetype of the wounded healer. This is one that keeps many among you in perpetual distress. The name perpetuates the idea that to do healing, the healer's wound must be fresh! There is little value that you can bring to a disturbed situation. In fact, when your wound is active you will be triggered and your perception may not be pure. The personal disruption must be calmed and cleared in you first, in order for you to bring value to others on any topic. Know that, as you do so, you are able to bring clarity and light.

Sisterhood © 2014 Claire Sierra

Chapter 8

Conclusion

Untangling

As you may have noticed, I struggled with my own perceptions and judgments about how this assignment should go. At times, I almost lost contact with the immense wisdom offered. I feared (often unconsciously) that I would be utterly changed and transformed by surrendering to this path, this process. Could I be brave enough to step into the potential that was being unveiled and offered to me? I feared scorn and ridicule for this writing. I've been surprised how dominating these subterranean thoughts could be. I learned that standing in one's divinely inspired purpose is not always easy. Encountering 4,000 years of culturally sanctioned gender oppression, violence, and negative conditioning (A.K.A. misogyny) requires steadfast courage and kindness to transmute. Dismantling the structures of our dominant culture's gender bias is a major renovation.

Paradoxically, there were also long nights when I worried that nothing of real merit was in these pages. It speaks to the deep discounting I've internalized about the importance of Feminine Soul. That perspective is bewildering to me now. I can't really explain my own blindness to the depth and beauty that was emerging right before my eyes. It's been an important (if not confounding) part of the journey. Graciously, I feel totally transformed and utterly inspired by this sparkling message for women in our new emerging world.

I share this so that as you discover your own beautiful, magical reality, you can expect twists and knots to untangle. Know that it is perfect, though often a winding path. This is a dance of Feminine Soul. The grace of transformation is a (sometimes maddening) process of meandering back and forth—remembering, forgetting, and remembering again. This beautiful architecture moves us into new layers within ourselves, into a new life. Trust the heart of your own process as you keep moving forward, confounding as it might be.

Opening Our Gifts

If you are at all like me, the forces that drive you are not always light, angelic, and airy-fairy. We learned that, in order to be successful, we had to put parts of ourselves away. We've been taught (trained, really) that our emotional, sensual, intuitive selves are messy and need to be contained and controlled. Our heart's clear wisdom has been subjugated to "superior" qualities of the mind: organization, logic, reason, and thinking. These aren't bad traits. And I'm not suggesting we give them up. There are sacred and practical qualities of the masculine. They're just not our only skills.

The driving thrum of "do more/have more" beats a compelling rhythm. The outer-world focus of the masculine can be so amazing, but also very distracting. So embedded in our culture, it's a challenge to pay attention to anything else sometimes. Masculine values beckon with needs, goals, and intentions that society has made so compelling. For women raised in this dominant style of doing and achieving, it almost takes an act of Goddess to divert our attention and focus within. There's a balance needed: creating enough structure (masculine) to keep things moving to completion, with enough creative space and flow (feminine) to allow intuition and grace. By integrating these two halves we are repairing, remembering, and becoming whole.

From Doing to Being

Since starting to write this book several years ago, I've seen a monumental shift in awareness of the Divine Feminine. While not a mainstream epidemic yet, I hear this theme discussed everywhere. I notice where the loss of the Feminine is woven into myriad social issues we are surrounded by, and how this reclamation is a solution to so many problems we face today.

We are bringing heart and Soul back into our decision-making to repair our stressed-out, overdrawn, dried up lives, as we revive ourselves and a teetering planet. What many of us (and our world at large) sorely need now are uniquely feminine abilities, kindled by our creative, connective Souls. In making this shift from mind-centered *doing* to heart-centered *being*, we meet a wiser, gentler, more intuitive self. We invent a life that is more organic, balanced, creative, and whole.

But sometimes what our hearts long for can seem so opposite from what society tells us we should want. As we turn within to the whispers of the heart—whether quiet or clamoring—and listen deeply, our holy desire comes out of hiding. This is a profound shift, and the inspired actions that result are amazingly productive in ways that the inner masculine self could never conjure. We still get things done, just without the usual way of pushing and driving. This is what the Feminine Soul shows us, when we let her. Our lives can flow, aligned with the cosmic forces of nature and the universal Source, God/Goddess.

Ultimately, this path is a call to create beauty, to ignite our immanence—using the energy of our Divine force *within* rather than exerting power *over*. It is an invitation to reunite the forces of the Divine Feminine with the Divine Masculine, balancing ourselves in this inner/outer dance of life. In order for this to happen, women need to have a solid Feminine center. We repair ourselves, and then re-pair with the masculine, so that these seeming opposites work in harmony—internally and in our world.

As you let your Soul steer your life, you allow inner guidance, intuition, and grace to lead. Previously unavailable or unrecognized connections, ideas, synchronicities and collaboration occur. From there, doing arises. It really does. It's a gentle but radical shift that takes courage, practice, and support. That is why this book is filled with skills, tools, and perspectives to guide you in this new way. This path is meant to be shared and explored with others; we no longer need to do it alone. I hope you've found that when you get into this flow, life works and can be fun, easy, relaxed, and light.

New Magdalene Sisters

Mary Magdalene: I bow to you, beloved.

Claire: And I you. Where shall we begin today?

Mary Magdalene: We hail and salute you. With this work, you are making the invisible visible "for those with ears to hear, and eyes to see." You are on the right track. The Divine Feminine is "hiding in plain sight." This is not just about me and my story, but rather a deeper message for women to relate to, about going into hiding for safety and then getting lost, invisible and forgotten along the way. Now it is time for you to find your way back to your true Divine selves. It is time for all women. You are now starting to carry Feminine Soul in a more potent way. Practice "shining." This is a part of what you are endeavoring to convey.

Claire: How am I to take this to the world?

Mary Magdalene: Call to the New Magdalene Sisters. You are offering a path to awaken the Divine Feminine. There are others on this path, some following this Magdalene mythos, others following different paths of purpose. You are all little pieces of a big puzzle. Some women will resonate with you, some with another. Though the language or framework may differ, the skills and tools are connected, one and the same, as we are all unwinding an old paradigm into a new one. There are levels that are like grades, for you are at different places along the path. This is important to recognize so not to discredit one as "above" or "below." You are all working to your level, and that is variable.

Remember your gift. That is the creative piece: the imaginal realm of art, imagery, movement, and meditation. The Soul calling for beauty. These are the skills you developed in order to be able to reach your people and lift your group. Others will be drawn to other methods and styles, and that is fine, too. There is no one ultimate Divine Feminine teaching—at least not from the vantage point of your culture now. It is a personal path, an uprising of energy that must be courted and cultivated.

These teachings will become more refined as they are worked into the population. There will start to be an emerging dialogue within the mainstream. We are not there yet, but it is moments away. Start to recognize this shift, to be able to cull and tend that conversation as it emerges more and more powerfully.

We are delighted with the progress you have made from just a week hence. We are also delighted that you are heeding the guidance to allow this process to be infused with joy.

Many women are remembering that this is something you all came here for, and chose to do. You are stepping up into this together, "up-drafting" with those of like mind. Birds of a feather flock together. This is how birds fly: each taking turns leading, lifting each other up, and riding drafts and pockets of upward-moving energy. The same is true for women: fly (work) together! That is a thrill as well, is it not?

Truly, let yourself enjoy your day as though you made it exactly as you planned—Heaven on Planet Earth—for you did. Why not celebrate this wondrous occurrence? Create and enjoy the output of your input (and vice versa).

Know that whenever you feel afraid, you can call me close. We, your guides and guardians, are working with you constantly. Feel the comfort wrapping your worries and then take the leap anyway. Listen to your ideas and inspiration, and trust that we are speaking to you as One. You are safe and will not be harmed. You are stronger than you give yourself awareness of and can handle small rejections better than you imagine. You are developing resiliency. With this comes the awareness that not everyone is your kindred and you are seeking those who are. They await you. So share this work: call them. We can speak more, but for now we are complete. Blessed be, good night.

Temple Time Returns

Women are hungry for change. Every day I meet women whose hearts are aching to live in deep peace, joy, and harmony within, then extending out to their neighbors, locally and globally. As feeling beings, we seem more attuned to the pain and suffering on the planet and are mobilizing internally, as well as in our own communities, to make needed changes.

We are creating a new world order, but not the one we hear about in the news. Women all over the world are emerging, creating a new culture to overlay and transform what we have now. We are feeling a longing, as we awaken old memories of a time and a place where women and feminine power were held sacred.

We are creating a new Divine archetype, and what this looks like is deeply personal for each of us. Some women relate to the Goddess in her various ancient manifestations. It's important to know that this lineage of female deities exists across cultures. Reflection on those ancient archetypes can be an excellent grounding point.

But for some women, these myths feel archaic and out of place in our modern lives. They feel contrived or a step backward in our socio-spiritual development. Goddesses of old are out of sync with emerging expressions of the Divine in all her/his forms. As we evolve, we look ahead. So while we can look to these myths and archetypes as guides, we must examine their relevance for the problems we face in the world today. We must take care not to lean so far backward that we trip on our nostalgia.

Instead, we move forward toward our own unique, personal and culturally relevant expression of the Sacred Feminine. We find the face of God who reflects our true radiance, as we begin to peek into the vast mystery and power that lives within us. It is time to remember and re-inhabit ourselves as Divine Feminine beings. As we do this, we undo old beliefs of "female" equaling heathen, stained at birth, impure, responsible for sin and damnation. We release any cellular memory of those absurd notions taught in the past.

A new mystery school is emerging, in which the secrets of the Divine Feminine sisterhood are being revealed. Ancient, native truth blends and merges with contemporary wisdom. We step into evolving levels of our own empowered, radiant co-creation. We experience the divinity of our true nature in our beautiful bodies, expansive minds, and creative spirits. Our holy moments have tears and laughter, sacred encounters and Soul-filled experiences. We live as if we are holy. We make magic happen.

As we do, we return to the temple, where Feminine wisdom reigns in our Queendom. This is no ancient myth; it is for our time, our era. Our mystery school is not bound by buildings or belief systems. It is not a dogma to join or a system to follow.

Temple Time is returning. But where is this Temple? It emerges from within each of us. The Temple is in the sanctuary of our lives, our homes, our hearts, our bodies, and our creative acts. The secrets of this sisterhood are not confined to a special time, place, or theology (though those are still lovely). Instead, Temple Time is woven into everyday life, as we experience our lives as unique, magical, and sacred. We live each moment as a prayer of hope and beauty.

This reclaimed refuge is still a hidden mystery to anyone who feels burned out, overwhelmed, exhausted, and invisible. This lifestyle dis-ease naturally leads to feeling out of balance, disconnected from our intrinsic wealth and divinity. We label and diagnose this culturally sanctioned pathology as insomnia, chronic fatigue, exhaustion, depression, anxiety, etc. And then we get on the hamster wheel, running to others for answers.

The wholeness we seek is not out there. It lives inside us, in our holy desires, creative acts, inspired dreams, and late-night longings. Now is the time for us to explore the depth and breadth of our own distinct mystery. As we do, we live into that place of embodied wisdom, rather than waiting for some authority figure to grant the right, prescription, or privilege to be whole and holy.

The day is here to know in our bones that we are holy. When we embody this truth, then our lives literally become pure magic. From this aligned, sacred center, everything changes. In partnership with the greater forces of the Universe (Source, God, Goddess, or whatever you call it), we can create anything we desire. That can mean bettering our own lives by manifesting great parking spots, nice cars, beautiful homes, and loving partnerships. But let's not stop there. There is a whole gorgeous world waiting to be reborn—a new earth that works for everyone, with abundance, harmony, peace, and joy for all. She's waiting for us to get it and get on it.

The Dalai Lama was quoted as saying, "The world will be saved by the Western women." When we have the inner and outer resources, we can make this happen. "We are the ones we have been waiting for," as the Hopi prophesy states. We can make it so. Life can be Heaven on Planet Earth when we allow it to be. Acting from this new truth of embodied, empowered, co-creative Feminine Soul, it emerges. This is the *real* new world order. Welcome home.

11 Keys to Awakening Feminine Soul

This whole book could be distilled into these eleven insights. Take on these simple (but not always easy!) perspectives as practices and change your life.

Feed the Feminine First[4]

Prioritize your Soul Care. Do the practices that bring direct contact with the Divine, early in your daily routine. Nurture your craving to express your Feminine essence sacredly. Act as if your silky, sweet, strong, sensuous self matters every day, because she does.

---
4 Thanks to Devaa Haley Mitchell for this gorgeous and empowering phrase.

Count Your Blessings

Gratitude and appreciation are the keys to happiness. By appreciating everything around you, more of this goodness will come. You cannot be grateful and unhappy at the same time. Try it; it's virtually impossible.

Lead with Intention

Your day (which becomes your life) is only as good as you imagine it to be. Take time to visualize how you'd like each aspect and interaction in your day to unfold for you. How big and juicy, easy and creative can you dream your life to be?

Cultivate Your Creative Center

Carve out time for nurturing acts of beauty and creative play. Find whatever that is for you: create art, write poetry, knit hats, grow vegetables, or cook a delicious meal. This is where the Divine Feminine lives, feeds, and flourishes.

Radiate Your Essence

Your true beauty shines from the inside out. Know your worth. Be the light you already are. Feel good being you and shine that out to the world around you. Radiance is a healing balm, it is powerful medicine.

Honor Your Body Temple

Take deep care of the physical being (that's you!) that carries your Spirit. Nurture yourself physically with exercise or activity that moves you, drink good clean flowing water, eat local organic whole foods, and bask in baths and the beauty of being outside.

Create Sacred Space

Express the true you. Let your home, wardrobe, and workplace be the Temple for your life. Cultivate beauty all around you, and it becomes you.

Listen to the Voice Within

Trust and act on your intuition. Learn to feel the difference between fear and guidance. This connection will grow in clarity and depth when you attend to it. Your inner wisdom knows your Soul purpose. Let your Soul shine.

Breathe

Bring in the light, especially whenever you're feeling stuck, stressed or stranded by life. This light (which is love or Source) is waiting to illuminate you. Relax then allow, feel, and observe. Energy will shift, change will come. Nothing stays the same. You can wait it out or make it better.

Ask for Help

Remember that you are always being divinely guided and protected. Take a quick, quiet moment and pray. Our Divine helpers cannot intervene without invitation. Neither will your friends or neighbors.

Embrace Your Perfect Now

What if this really *is* Heaven on Planet Earth? Live your life with the absolute belief that you are exactly who and where you are supposed to be, having the perfect experience. Life is always working for the best and highest, for the good of all beings (even when there's evidence to the contrary). Accept what is and then start to make upgrades. Living from this knowing will rock your world.

Magdalene Speaks

As I rounded the bend towards completion of this sacred guidebook, I wondered what Magdalene's perspective might be. She offered this early on, and as I came across it again, it seems to be the perfect summary.

Mary Magdalene: For women, to reclaim the Divine Feminine is to reveal the sacred within. A woman with a revived inner feminine has a sense of herself as whole and holy. She is held by God, and knowing that she is part of and connected to this sacredness, she is sacred. Which is why awakening the Feminine Soul is such deep and important work.

Women are now ready to reveal their true divinity to themselves and to the world. And the world is ready. The world needs all the self-expressed, inspired, confident, love-filled women who are ready to live as a force to be reckoned with. This is not angry and aggressive, but a strong, fierce, vibrant force of love, that is a gentle, warm breeze at the end of a long, hot summer day. The world needs this love and the cleansing force it implies. Prepare yourself. This wind is gathering power and coming your way.

Imbue Magic into Every Day

I invite you to begin (or continue) the journey of accessing the feminine half of the Divine partnership. You are a Goddess. Reclaim your rightful place in the pantheon of Heaven. It is time for the Divine divorce to end. Know your full power and grace now.

From this place of immanence—in awakened, embodied Goddesshood—you can begin to create the shifts you know are necessary, but might previously have thought impossible. This empowered vision is imperative for life on planet Earth today. With economic, environmental and social crises heating up around the globe this seems more important now than ever. You see it, sense it, and feel it everywhere. It is time to knock the sleep of old paradigm, mechanistic materialism from your eyes and wake up. You don't have to, you *get* to.

Unlock this awareness and embody your Divine self. Imbue magic into the physical reality of daily life. You can birth your creative genius into a myriad of forms. The tools, skills, practices, and perspectives shared in these pages are designed to support your expansion. As you dream a bigger, brighter vision, your image of the future transforms and with it, so does your life. What an exciting time to be alive. The Divine Feminine is waking up through you and as you. Wow, are you gorgeous, Goddess.

Next Steps on The Path

If the magic of *The Magdalene Path* has captivated you, I welcome you. Please know you don't have to do this alone. I want to remind you to seek out others to share your journey. I invite you (if you have not done so already) to join the community of women (and men) who are unveiling the Sacred Feminine and exploring the priestess path through Mary Magdalene.

Deepen your experience by visiting MagdalenePath.com, where you will find countless resources for your reflection and enjoyment. The practices in this book are available at the website as a separate workbook, so you can journal and take notes, without writing in the book (super helpful for e-book readers and library users.) You can review the skills and practices easily. There are also recordings of meditations from this book, along with new articles and other resources—including updated information about gatherings, groups, free teleseminars and other kinds of events. And other gorgeous surprises to come!

Welcome, sister. This path is deep and wide, there is room for you here. Please join me.

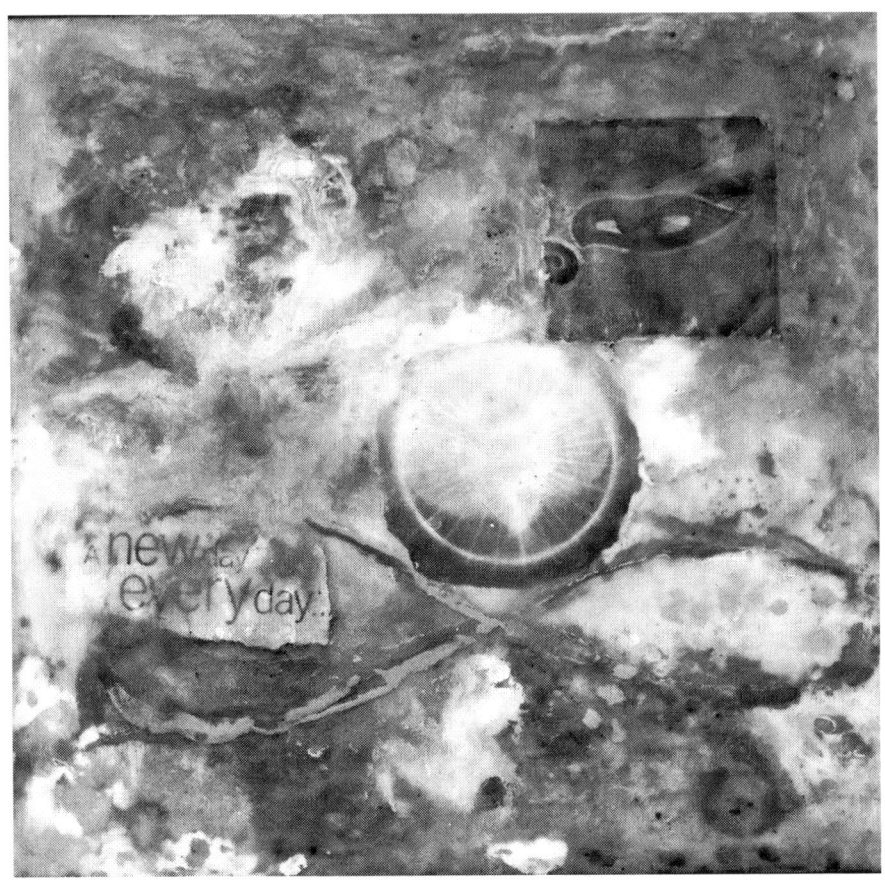

New Day © 2014 Claire Sierra

Appendix 1:

Re-visioning Mary Magdalene

It's become apparent to me as I've shared *The Magdalene Path* that my interest in Mary Magdalene is not unique as I had once thought. There is something compelling and mysterious about her. Over the course of developing this manuscript, I've had the good fortune to enjoy countless discussions with men and women who are interested in her "real story." Some were raised with the Catholic understanding of her, as I was. Others with different religious backgrounds (or none at all) have no clear idea of who she is, yet they are curious about this woman of intrigue who walked closely with Jesus. Women sense that she has meaning and mythos for us as "the other Mary." Many wonder, as I did, if something was missing or askew in the mainstream understanding of her role in the Christian story. We hunger for the Truth.

The main areas of confusion and inquiry about Mary Magdalene seem to be her name, her role or position, and her relationship with Jesus. Was she actually his wife? Did they have children? Did she go to France as legends say? These questions are actually connected, intertwined with power and politics as much as religion and spirituality.

Since I am not an academic and don't pretend to be a biblical scholar, I have always avoided presenting historical information about the life of Mary Magdalene. There are a few reasons for this. First, I'm not great at holding facts, dates, and details of that sort. And there is so much conflicting information and opinion. Also, growing up Catholic, I don't have a good understanding of (or interest in) the Bible, the source of these stories. Even with the changes of Vatican II, this was absent from my education and upbringing—we were to listen to the priests and follow their doctrine. We were not really encouraged to gather information or opinions ourselves. And finally, *The Magdalene Path* is not about facts and figures or rewriting Biblical history. This is about us reclaiming something that was lost (or taken). But I have explored Magdalene's life for some time and as I get asked questions about her, I recognize misconceptions that need to be clarified.

There are some basic understandings that I have come to hold as Truth that are important reframes of the classic story we've been told. I want to provide a sketch to get you started. By no means is this meant to be an exhaustive review of literature. Should you require more details, please see my resources cited in the bibliography below. In the end, you will still need to make your own choices about who to believe and what feels true.

Often I read incorrect references regarding her moniker, Mary Magdalene. She is erroneously referred to as Mary of Magdala, as though she comes from a town of that name. Interestingly, the location known as Magdala was not called that during her lifetime. Also, women of that era were not known by place names. Instead, in the culture of that time, they were generally identified by their husband's name. An example of this is Mary Cleopas, who was the wife of Cleopas.

Instead, Magdalene appears to be a title coming out of the sacred Hebrew texts, which Christians refer to as the Old Testament. The title *Magdalene* references prophesy from the book of Micah (4:8-11), regarding the *Magdal-eder*, which means "watchtower of the flock." *Magdala* means "high, watchtower, citadel, or fortress" in Aramaic, which would be indicative of a leadership role, appropriate for a High Priestess or spiritual teacher. Margaret Starbird beautifully elaborates on this in her work. By denying Mary Magdalene this title, she is stripped of her leadership position in the church hierarchy. I see this as intentional—what we name things (or people) directly impacts what and how we think of them. By correcting this misunderstanding about her name as a title, she is returned to a place of position, honor and power.

The four main books of the Christian New Testament (Matthew, Mark, Luke, and John) refer to several women named Mary, and other women in key moments are entirely unnamed, so it can be hard to tell one from the other. This creates great ambiguity about the role of Mary the Magdalene. Research indicates that Mary of Bethany (notice she is never "Mary Bethany"), Mary the sister of Martha and Lazarus, and the woman with the alabaster jar who anointed Jesus' head with nard (or spikenard) were one and the same: Mary Magdalene.

Why is there all the confusion about her name and identity? Several possibilities. First, the Jewish sacred texts (commonly referred to as the "Old Testament") were passed as oral tradition for hundreds of years before being written in Hebrew, which was the temple language of the rabbis. The spoken language was Aramaic. The holy Christian texts (or "New Testament") were originally penned in Greek, translated to Latin, and then finally into Shakespeare's Old English. No wonder these stories are so hard to understand! Until the invention of the printing press, they were hand-transcribed by monks, so just imagine the glitches in translation.

Secondly, the Gospels of Matthew, Mark, Luke, and John are the four main, official (or "canonical") books of the Bible's New Testament. Scholars say they were written between 35-75 years after the time of Jesus—that's two or three generations after his lifetime. Paul's letters were written earlier (40 years after Jesus' death) when he was in Greece—and he never met Jesus, either. Therefore, these are not eyewitness accounts but scribed from oral tradition and memory. Most people were illiterate during that time, so storytelling was a major source of education. Given that time gap, it would be easy to confuse and conflate the names and details of these stories.

Different personal religious and political power agendas were at play as the disciples went into the world to share their "Good News." That ministry also harbored different opinions about the role of women (especially Mary Magdalene). Jesus was a maverick for treating women as equals, traveling and talking with them. This was not the norm of Hebrew culture at the time and his attitude was not shared by all his disciples.

Recall the great danger in being a follower of Jesus after his death, which would have obscured or skewed the stories. On top of that, add the fact that if Mary Magdalene was carrying Jesus' child, his heir, it would be important to protect them both. Some followers wanted to keep her and the bloodline of Jesus hidden while retaining the spiritual teachings she held. Others wanted to forget her and move into their own positions of power. Whether intention or accidental, she was so well hidden she was eventually forgotten and misrepresented.

The primary misconception regarding the Magdalene concerns her identity as a prostitute. This misinterpretation has created the greatest damage to her character, since it is the main "fact" that most people know. Ironically, nowhere in the Bible does it name Mary Magdalene as a whore, and yet centuries of misinformation carry this forward to this day. The

Bible does mention her more than any other woman but never does it identify her vices or name her as a prostitute. She is noted in all gospels as a leader and a woman of wealth who sponsored Jesus' healing entourage financially. Interesting how that piece of lore gets lost in transmission!

Many are unaware of the fact that in 1969, during the restructuring of Vatican II, the Catholic church recanted their position that Magdalene was a prostitute. Her ill-repute can be traced to a series of famous (but inaccurate) sermons given by Pope Gregory, in 591 C.E., (Common Era) which went unchecked for centuries. This influential pontiff created official church doctrine out of an unsanctioned view of her story. He created a negative image of her (and women in general) and his sermons became treated as gospel truth. Since most people at the time were illiterate, educated solely by stories and lectures such as these, only the elite few had access to the source documents to corroborate that information. With that, Mary Magdalene's conflicted image was solidified for nearly 1400 years.

Naming her as a "fallen woman" (rather than a leader) served to discredit her and radically reduced her role in the sacred drama that was being played out. It also seemed to have a larger political and social impact by denigrating the role of women in the church hierarchy and society in general. As a female mentor during a time of uncertainty and unrest among the religious leadership following Jesus' death, certainly she would have been seen as a threat. And if she was a priestess, her temple practices would have been seen by the ruling religious elite as threatening, at best and blasphemously unholy, at worst.

As an interesting side note, Magdalene has long been revered in France. Legend has it that she landed in the south of France, in a town now called Saintes Maries De La Mer (Saints Marys of the Sea) near Marseille. France has numerous holy sites devoted to Magdalene that pilgrims still visit today. She was well venerated throughout France in all the cathedrals devoted to "Our Lady" (Notre Dame) until the 1200s. During this time the Albigensian Crusade eradicated almost 1 million Cathars who practiced another version of Christianity. Coincidentally, there was a transition to the veneration of Mother Mary as the Blessed Virgin and Madonna in these locations, right at this same time. All the grand cathedrals (and their Black Madonna statues of the dark, hidden Goddess) were originally devoted to Magdalene! She is still present there in paintings, stained glass, and statuary—hiding in plain sight!

Uncovering these and other clues, researchers find information "hiding in plain sight" embedded in the Christian Bible by comparing it to customs and historical data from that era. Looking at the culture of that time, Hebrew men were married by the age of 20 and would leave the family home. For Jesus to be respected as a teacher (called "rabbi") and leader of the Jews, he would have to follow that tradition. For him to be unmarried as a rabbi in his 30s would defy Jewish law and was so highly unusual that it would have been noteworthy. Nowhere does it say he was a bachelor. Yet, the Catholic practice of celibacy for priests is based on the assertion of his single status. (Interestingly, however, this tradition was not instituted until the 800s.)

Scholars note that the four Gospels of Matthew, Mark, Luke, and John seem to borrow from each other (at times almost word for word) while at others they contradict each other entirely. One of the only stories mentioned in all four books of the New Testament was the anointing of Jesus' head with sacred ointment. This action was symbolic and was recognized as the fulfillment of prophesy that Jesus was messiah. Anointing with oil was an ancient sacred ritual of kingship and marriage practiced throughout the Middle East for centuries. This practice, rich with symbolism, would have been clearly understood at that time. Since

Jesus Christ means "Jesus, the Anointed One," (in Greek) this sacred activity is obviously significant. And Jesus is often referred to as the bridegroom, but where is the bride? The anointer, by tradition, was always his bride. While the moment was noted, the importance and identity of the bride was conveniently omitted.

So who would Jesus have been married to? If we look, there is only one woman in the biblical stories who travels with Jesus and is present at his ritual marriage, king-making, subsequent death, and resurrection. Though the details vary, they all point to Mary Magdalene as his forgotten beloved. Jesus said when the anointing story is retold, it will be "in memory and honor of her"—the anointer as well as the anointed one. He clearly saw the importance.

Magdalene's role is also clear during the death of Jesus. When the disciples of Jesus abandoned him at the hour of mortal danger, she along with his mother, Mary, stayed with him even at the Crucifixion. She was present at the tomb after his burial, the first person to whom Jesus appeared after his resurrection. Telling the others of the "good news" of that miracle, she was named "the Apostle to the Apostles."

We can also look to other biblical sources from that era for clues about Mary Magdalene. The Bible has not always been in the current form that we know today. Many other Gospels and sacred books were removed from the New Testament during the Council of Nicaea. In 325 C.E., this group, led by Emperor Constantine, molded church doctrine and coalesced political power in the Roman empire.

Later, church leaders created doctrines of celibacy for Jesus as the basis for the same in priesthood—what a disaster that has been. They manufactured virginity for his mother, another Mary, despite her having at least one son and daughter mentioned in the Bible. (Virgin, by the way, originally meant "whole of herself," having more to do with personal sovereignty than sexual purity.) This effectively left the Magdalene out of the picture almost entirely.

In recent years, Mary Magdalene's role is being reexamined, as Gospels that were removed from the Bible (the Gospels of Mary, Philip and Thomas, and others) are being re-discovered. In 1945, the Nag Hammadi library was found in the desert of Egypt by a Bedouin nomad. Twelve leather-bound papyrus documents were hidden in earthen jars around 400 C.E., probably so that the owners would avoid persecution by the official Christian church of the Roman Empire. These parchments show a different version of early Christianity than mainstream religious traditions and point to fundamental differences in beliefs and practices than are widely known today.

The Gnostic Gospels (from *"gnosis,"* which means inner knowledge, enlightenment, or "Oneness with God") of the early Christian era reveal a very different view of Mary Magdalene, Jesus, and his ministry. These books reveal some of the power and leadership struggles of early Christianity toward Mary Magdalene. From sacred texts such as the Gospels of Philip and Thomas, it seems that her status as the "apostle to the apostles," in the post Jesus era created jealousy among the twelve apostles, particularly Peter. The controversy stemmed from the intimacy of her relationship with Jesus, which in some accounts included being cited as his favorite, loved more than the rest, and appeared to have had a physical aspect that included kissing.

New evidence is being presented that she was indeed the sacred partner to Jesus. Other passages indicate that she had deeper knowledge and shared practices with Jesus that the others were not privy to. Early Christian writers understood the archetypal role Magdalene held as an incarnation of "holy wisdom" and named her as bride to Jesus the Christ.

Despite these golden threads elevating her status in the earliest Christian records of the third and through fourth centuries, an elaborate tapestry was woven of Mary Magdalene as a repentant prostitute-sinner. Confusion attached to Mary Magdalene's character was compounded across time and twisted accordingly. On that falsehood a powerful position was developed that used her fabricated legend to discredit her and thus disempower women and our sensuality/sexuality in general.

The conflicts that define the Christian church can all be viewed as second chakra issues and attitudes toward the material world: homosexuality, priest's celibacy, sexual abuse scandals, women's ordination, and the authority of an all-male clergy. These relate back to the denial of the feminine in Magdalene's unacknowledged position within the formative Christian community. Her role as a feminine advisor, along with her body, sensuality, and sexuality were seen as dangerous to church dogma by virtue of her being female and were used as tools to damage our memory of her. And because any theological diversity was branded as heresy, (punishable by death), the primary misinterpretation of Mary Magdalene was impossible to revise. By discrediting her, she was marginalized and removed.

But what is hidden is not necessarily lost. Instead, her memory is sprouting up and very much alive. Archeologists, historians, academics and interested others are discovering more about her and her cohorts through the Canonical and Gnostic Gospels as well as other ancient texts which seem to be unearthed more and more frequently.

Where does all this lead us and why is it important? If biblical scholars and historians are correct, a vastly inaccurate, incomplete version of Christianity has been passed down to us. Whether this was intentional or accidental, the result slanted our culture radically away from male-female balance, partnership and feminine leadership toward masculine primacy.

In losing Magdalene as the bride, beloved and partner of Jesus, we lost the marriage and sacred union (known in ancient times as "Hieros Gamos") of two equal partners. Instead, we were shown a single man who was a God—someone we could try, but never live up to—the sole offspring of a male God. We have a holy trinity of masculine power. This lop-sided cosmology impacts our consciousness and how we view the world. We see the consequences in all areas of society, effecting culture throughout the world in politics, commerce, spirituality, personal relationships and the environment. With Christianity (and other male-centric religions) being such a dominant force throughout the world, it impacts our lives in ways we barely see, like a fish in water. ("What water?")

One day we may know the "true story" of Jesus or Mary Magdalene from a fully documented, historical perspective. There is vast, varied and conflicted opinion where these matters are concerned. History is always written by the winners, shaped by the era as well one's perspective because of age, class, gender and life experiences that form opinion. That's only natural. Now we are in a time when we can do our own exploring and discover. Use discernment and draw your own conclusions. Ultimately we are each responsible for our own Truth.

Resources

The practices and perspectives offered in the book are available as a **free downloadable workbook**. Please go to MagdalenePath.com.

Additionally if you are interested in **book club questions** for personal use or group study, please see the resources section of the website, where you can download them for use. There you can learn about joining a book club, along with engaging in groups, programs, teleconference calls and other events that will support your connection to Mary Magdalene and awakening your Divine Feminine Essence. You can find out about these and more at MagdalenePath.com

In addition to the tools and processes in this book, here are a few others I use on a regular basis for myself and my clients. I am not endorsing these, nor am I offering these as medical advice, treatment or diagnosis. These are for your personal growth and enjoyment only. Check them out and see if you find them helpful or supportive. Please consult your healthcare practitioner before initiating any of these techniques.

The Belief Closet - Belief change and clearing process working with unconscious imagery and the imaginal realm. Highly effective and fun. www.TransformYourBeliefs.com

Bliss Breakthrough – In-person and virtual programs to support successful professional women to recover from exhaustion, burnout, overwhelm and chronic fatigue so they can reclaim their juicy creativity, feminine essence, vitality, and sensuality. www.BlissBreakthrough.com

EFT - Emotional Freedom Technique A.K.A. Tapping, is a Meridian Tapping Therapy that clears the body's energy field of it's physical, mental and emotional constrictions that lead to pain and illness. www.TheTappingSolution.com or www.EmoFree.com

The Emotion Code - Identifies and clears old emotions that become trapped in your body-mind system and then hamper your current life experience. www.theemotioncode.com or www.drbradleynelson.com/

Feminine Power - Increase women's empowerment through tools and practices to support living bigger dreams. www.FemininePower.com

Menstrual Health Foundation (later **New Cycle Products** and **Womankind**) - Products and services that teach women to honor their fertility cycle through fertility and cycle awareness, menstrual health products, rites of passage workshops and ceremonies for coming of age and menopause. This organization was the brainchild of evolutionary artist/educator, Tamara Slayton, who passed away in 2003. http://sophiainstitute.us/onlineFSC/TamaraSlayton.htm

The Fertility Deva, The Red Tent and **The Red Web** - These organizations carry on the spirit of Tamara's work with young and mature women. http://holisticsexed.com/, www.deannalam.com/ or www.theredweb.org.

Tomar Levine - Akashic Record Readings woven with skillful and intuitive coaching for spiritual entrepreneurs. www.SoulGuidanceForYourBusiness.com.

True Purpose Process - An innovative set of tools and processes to find and live one's life purpose. TruePurposeInstitute.com

Reference

If you wish to dive into the life of Mary Magdalene a little more, here are some books and websites that have informed my consciousness for years. This is by no means an exhaustive list or a complete review of literature on the topic. There are new books and websites about Magdalene appearing all the time, so this is not intended to be definitive. Please know that while these have been helpful to my journey, I am not endorsing any of these as Truth (that is your own search), nor do I wish to discredit any source that is omitted.

Books

Barnstone, Willis, ed., *The Other Bible*

Bradley, Marion Zimmer, *Mists of Avalon, Priestesses of Avalon, Forest House*

*Calhoun, Flo Aeveia Magdalena, *I Remember Union*

Cunningham, Elizabeth, *The Return of the Goddess*

Diamant Anita, *The Red Tent*

*Douglas-Klotz, Neil, *Prayers of the Cosmos*

Freke, Timothy & Peter Gandy, *Jesus and the Lost Goddess*

Harvey, Andrew & Anne Baring, *The Divine Feminine*

Haskins, Susan, *Mary Magdalene: Myth and Metaphor*

Houston, Siobhan, *Invoking Mary Magdalene*

Kenyon, Tom and Judi Sion, *The Magdalen Manuscript*

*Kinstler, Clysta, *The Moon Under Her Feet*

Le Loup, Yves, *The Gospel of Mary Magdalene*

Malachi, Tau, *Living Gnosis*

*McGowan, Kathleen, The Magdalene Line Series: *The Expected One, The Book of Love* and *The Poet Prince; The Source of Miracles*

*Miller, Ruth L., *Mary's Power, Notre Dame* and others

Norton, Joan & Margaret Starbird, *14 Steps to Awaken the Sacred Feminine*

*Starbird, Margaret, *Woman with the Alabaster Jar, Goddess in the Gospels* and others

Walker, Barbara, *The Women's Encyclopedia of Myths and Secrets*

* These authors were particularly important and defining in my exploration.

Websites

One could spend hours (and I have) surfing the web to find compelling information on Mary Magdalene and the Divine Feminine. This is so much simpler than traveling hither and yon to esoteric centers, academic and spiritual libraries (which I also have done, in the pre-internet days.) Here are some websites with interesting and helpful resources. Use your own discernment, always.

Divine Feminine and Mary Magdalene book, artwork, programs, resources, blog, and newsletter: TheMagdalenePath.com/ Join the Facebook group: Magdalene Path at https://www.facebook.com

Women's Empowerment, Soul Care and Creative Arts: www.BlissBreakthrough.com

Nag Hammadi Library: www.gnosis.org/naghamm/nhl.html

Gnostic Gospels of Mary, et al.: www.gnosis.org/library/marygosp.htm

Alternative information and resources about Jesus and Mary Magdalene, medieval myths and contemporary lore: www.thetruejesus.org/mary.htm

General Mary Magdalene information, with articles from well-known writers: www.magdalene.org/mmcontent/articles.htm

http://www.smithsonianmag.com/history-archaeology/magdalene.html#ixzz2YDRr51o4

Esoteric spiritual teaching, Celtic lore and Magdalene mysteries: www.northernway.org/mmag.html

About the Author

Claire Sierra, M.A. is a transformational counselor who has helped thousands of women overcome depression, anxiety, overwhelm and burnout to step into their clarity and joy. For over 22 years, this inspiring Soul coach has led hundreds of creative and inspiring workshops, retreats, teleseminars, and private sessions across the country, helping people access their divine connection and Soul purpose through creative arts.

Trained as an Expressive Arts Therapist and True Purpose™ Master Coach, Claire uses cutting edge practices that fit her grounded, expansive, soulful approach. She has maintained a private therapy practice for over 17 years and worked as an Art Therapist and Counselor at treatment centers, community agencies, and hospitals. As director of **Bliss Breakthrough,** Claire offers in-person and virtual retreats, coaching groups, teleseminars, and private sessions. She is a widely published author who has contributed to wellness magazines for decades. As a visionary mixed media artist, Claire has exhibited art in museums and galleries, now held in collections throughout the U.S.

Visit her website: BlissBreakthrough.com for free resources including a free Bliss Breakthrough Guided Meditation recording and a report, "Six Key Tools to Relieve Burnout, Exhaustion and Overwhelm." You will also receive her monthly newsletter. Visit MagdalenePath.com for free resources including access to meditations, teleseminars, virtual and in-person retreats.

The Magdalene Path

Book Club

Want to know more? Engage with like-minded Souls who are on a similar journey of exploration and expression into the path of the Magdalene and the Divine Feminine.

Join a Magdalene Path Book Club.

Whether you have a book club, women's group or sister circle already formed, or are looking for one to join, go to MagdalenePath.com.

Look for the downloadable *Magdalene Path Book Club Study Guide* complete with questions and activities to further your exploration.

Join the Facebook group and like the page: Magdalene Path at https://www.facebook.com/TheMagdalenePath and get in the conversation! Ask questions and communicate with others on this path. Find out about upcoming Magdalene Path events.

Connect with a community of sisters (and brothers, men are welcome) exploring this new paradigm in women's creativity and spirituality.

Printed in Great Britain
by Amazon